Celibacy: Renewing the Gift, Releasing the Power

Raymond J. Gunzel

Sheed & Ward

Sheed & Ward™ is a service of National Catholic Reporter Publishing
Company, Inc.

Library of Congress Catalog Card Number: 88-61680

ISBN: 1-55612-197-0

Published by: Sheed & Ward
115 E. Armour Blvd. P.O. Box 419492
Kansas City, MO 64141-6492

To order, call: (800) 333-7373

Contents

Foreword

During the course of writing this book, I had many occasions to ask myself why I had chosen to write on celibacy. Aren't there more pressing issues in the Church and the World? In fact, isn't celibacy too circumscribed in its appeal to the Christian community? Certainly there would be advantages to writing on issues that speak to a wider audience about a more relevant social concern. However, after reflecting on these questions I was convinced that celibacy is quite pertinent to some of the more dramatic issues facing the Church and the world today. Yes, there are many pressing social and religious matters crying out for attention, but, to me, the issue of celibacy as it pertains to the quality of life and human relationships, as well as to the quality of the Church's prophetic presence in modern society, seems of paramount importance.

The fundamental premise of this book is uncomplicated and straightforward: Either celibacy works for us or it works against us. It brings spiritual life to its fullness or it brings spiritual death. There is no middle ground. True celibates must be totally engaged in a relationship with the Divine and given over to the task of realizing the Kingdom in the course of human history.

The message of this book stands unabashedly on the notion that celibacy can be a living and creative experience only when it is grounded in contemplative prayer. Such prayer, when it is real and rooted at the center of our being, will lead to an opening and unfolding of our consciousness to an awareness of God—living, present, and active in the course of our individual lives, and through our lives active in the course of history.

Unless celibacy leaves us open to a personal and intimate relationship with the living God, we cave in on ourselves and become the embodiment of the very values and conventions we are called to stand against. In this case, celibacy is no more than merely a state of being unmarried, free to pursue our own whims and fancies. We join the unenlightened masses of swinging, upwardly mobile singles, perpetually imprisoned in a compulsive drive for adolescent self-gratification.

The gift of celibacy can be called forth as a living and creative presence of the Church in the world only through the reestablishment of contemplative prayer as the primary and foundational value in all Christian vocations.

Contemplation—and the mystical awareness that is its fruit—needs to be pulled out of the closet of history and reinserted in its proper place in daily life and worship, not only for priests and religious, but for the laity as well. Contemplative prayer, with an abiding awareness of God living and present in our lives, is the cornerstone upon which Christian worship—I dare say all worship—revolves. If the church is to take its place as a prophetic presence in modern society, challenging, judging, confronting, and calling history and the human enterprise back to its true path under the guidance of Divine Wisdom, that will happen only because the faithful people who comprise her body, live with their hearts grounded in an awareness of the promises of God being fulfilled in contemporary daily life.

Celibate presence in the Church can be the living center where this process of return begins, because the celibate, grounded in a life of faith, prayer, and the Evangelical Counsels, has nothing to lose, nothing to gain save the Kingdom for which he or she has left everything.

In this treatise I have attempted to focus entirely on the issue of celibacy as an expression of one's relatedness to God, who enters into and accompanies the unfolding of history through the mediation of human instruments. The key factor in this relationship is not one's perfection, virtue, or holiness in the popular sense of these words. Union with God depends far more on a readiness to be drawn into the divine plan from within our broken condition and propensity to sin. This is the truest meaning of "holy obedience," the obedience that heeds the call to live totally in the light of God's will without counting the cost. Thus celibacy, seen and understood within the context of authentic faith, is a surrender of one's life to unmediated union with the source and the end of all life through contemplation and a living out of the fruits of contemplation.

While psychology, sociology, and modern pedagogy have provided us with insights that deepen our understanding of psychosexual processes, they do not and cannot accompany us in a unique, mysterious encounter with the God who created us and confronts us within the mystery of our sinful but always unfolding lives. Such an encounter can take place only in the realm of pure faith for which there is no substitute.

This, I fear, is where most of our attempts to form young people for a life of celibacy and to minister to the wounded celibate fall short. Even our so-called Christian therapeutic endeavors and formation policies seem, at times, to be no more than rational scientific methodologies with a veneer of religious jargon and a smattering of pious devotional practices. Carl Jung cautioned would-be psychoanalysts that they could not hope to accompany their clients to where they themselves had never been. How weighty, then, is the responsibility of the Christian teacher or healer to be aware of and personally grounded in a living faith in the inherent and ineradicable goodness of the human person and in the participation of human life in the eternal and infinite source of all life.

If, in our formation or therapeutic programs, the Christian teacher or therapist does no more than put a layer of worldly sophistication over shallow, conventional religiosity, superimposing contemporary psychological methods and proceedures, then the objects of those efforts will receive no more than that which limited human knowledge and experience have to offer. Likewise, the most profound and insightful psychology and pedagogy, combined with the most skilled methodology, will be able to do little more than bring those people to an uneasy truce with the mystery of their lives in the face of the exigencies of conventional value systems. For them the standard for behaviour is grounded in conventional norms of society, not the mystery of the *imago dei* coming to be in each person even while he or she may be enmeshed in the futility of human weakness and sin. A living, dynamic faith and a knowing based on one's personal encounter with the Living God are the sources of redemptive growth and healing that Christian therapists and teachers can offer to the Body of Christ. This applies especially to all who are engaged in the selection, formation, and training of candidates for a life of celibacy. "We cannot give what we do not have" is a timeworn expression, but it is no less true for all its tiredness.

Because I want to address the issues of celibacy from the point of view of faith in the Judeo-Christian spirituality, I have chosen not to deal explicitly with such problem areas as homosexuality, pedophilia, or other types of troubling behaviour that are attracting attention today. Such types of behaviour are symptomatic of a much larger and, I believe, much more critical problem for the Church. At the risk of oversimplifying this enormously complex problem, I submit there is a twofold aspect, centered on the issue of faith. Our faith in God is a mirror image of our faith in ourselves and of our belief in the underlying goodness of creation as a manifestation of the wisdom of God. Conversely, when we see large-scale cynicism about the dignity and promise of the human person, we know that our faith in God as a living source of strength and wisdom has been seriously eroded. Then faith in God becomes largely reduced from living experience

to abstract sepculation and dry dogma . We attempt to manage human behaviour by law and by socioreligious convention. Thus we keep things
tidy on a superficial level, but the underside of the reality is that we lose
sight of our call to transformation and union with God. As a result, we are
enormously successful in bringing forth a community of people frozen into
socioreligious conformity. Truly free, spontaneous, and wise persons
grounded in an awareness of their unique relationship with a God of love
are increasingly rare.

Today, hope in the promise of humanity has largely given way to
cynicism and despair over our inability to conquer greed, lust, and violence
in order to live in Godlike relationships. Humanity has lost sight of the
reality of its divine origin and destiny. Perhaps the sin of our day is
"spiritual amnesia." We simply don't know who we are. The teaching
church, from the Pope and the Roman Curia all the way to Christians at the
grass roots level, must take its share of the blame for failing to proclaim
the primordial truth of divine revelation. For too many of us, religion has
become a dull and tedious round of ritual actions and codified beliefs
having little or nothing to do with encountering a god who calls us into the
divine-human adventure of guiding history and creation to their appointed
end. Or, perhaps worse, religion has become merely the reinforcement of
unredeemed values and beliefs enabling us to remain comfortable and
secure in a society, the continued existence of which depends on sustaining
unjust and oppressive structures. Pop psychology and self-help formulas
for instant happiness, all promising a utopia of self-actualization, have
taken the place of the way of the Cross, of self-realization in the truth of
God, and of Christ-centered relationships.

Looking at the more deeply underlying issues of faith, prayer, and
prophetic action does not lead to immediate surface solutions that will grat-
ify our need for control and a sense of accomplishment. But I believe that
such an approach will begin to reawaken us to a realization of what God
has wrought in our past and rekindle our hope in the continuing possibility
of that ongoing, creative-redemptive process happening in our lives. We
need to believe with boldness and to proclaim the Good News with the
original enthusiasm of Pentecost.

A strand of belief that runs throughout this book is that no matter what the quality and condition of one's relationship with self and others, each life—with all its unfathomable mystery—is the object of God's unqualified and unconditional mercy and redeeming love. There is not one life, no matter how enmeshed in sin and brokenness, that cannot—will not—be raised to the heights of prophetic witness and personal, unmediated union with God, provided that he is allowed to enter.

Another underlying theme of this book is the belief that much of our Western Christian spirituality, and thus, our corresponding attitudes towards sexuality and celibacy, is sown in tainted soil.

Because of a wide variety of historical circumstances, not the least of which is the pervasive influence of Platonic duality, Judeo-Christian spirituality, most notably as it has been developed in the West, has been uprooted from its biblical origins. Instead of celebrating our humanity and creation as the fundamental sacraments of God's action in wisdom and goodness, we struggle against deep seated fears and suspicions of our human nature. Instead of seeing in creation and the unfolding of history the arena in which we are called to cooperate in bringing about the reign of Divine wisdom and justice, we find ourselves subtly influenced by an attitude that seeks to diminish history and creation as at least irrelevant, and at most obstacles to be overcome in our search for true peace.

To be in an adversarial stance with our human nature, to be in an aggressive, consuming stance with material creation and the historical process, is to be alienated from the very point at which God wishes to be revealed and engaged in cooperative action.

One of the most fundamental needs of the Church in our time is a radical conversion to the Gospel as the fundamental standard of our Christian life and worship expressed in action. This implies a bold and fearless admission of the elements in our present day practices and beliefs that are contrary to the spirit of Revelation.

The conversion process begins with each and every person. As we become more at home with our humanity, are able to celebrate all of creation in sacraments and worship, there will unfold a more gracious, welcoming openness to the mystery of God self-revealing and self-giving in our enfleshed lives.

Contemplative prayer, healthy Christian asceticism, an affirmative, faithful supporting community grounded in a belief and hope in the goodness of one another—in spite of evidence to the contrary—are components that will lead to a real, experiential encounter with a God who lives, creates and redeems, even in the crunch of earthy human endeavor.

This modest effort at publishing could never have come this far were it not for the encouragement and support of a great number of friends and associates who were generous beyond the call of duty in lending time and talents in reading, criticizing and generally encouraging the work.

Most especially am I indebted to Christina Spahn and Margaret Kutcher. Without their steady prodding and encouragement, this effort would have mired down long ago. The two of them were tireless in reading and rereading the manuscript through its many revisions. Never did they hesitate, never did they tire. Each careful reading brought forth new observations and suggestions that greatly enhanced the quality and style of the work. Christina's years as a religious educator and adult Religious Education Coordinator enabled her to offer valuable and original suggestions concerning many theological points. Margaret's sharp eye and critical mind never tired of seeing new possibilities for style and arrangement of material.

With all its very evident faults and shortcomings, the effort has been enriched by their generous efforts. The publication of this work is a testimony to their gracious generosity.

1

Putting the Issue into Perspective

Chastity and virginity have been cherished and revered in the Christian community since the very first days of the post-Resurrection Church. While the rationale and motivation for their practice have changed with the epochs of history and the development of theological understanding, these virtues have remained, at least in theory, highly esteemed by the Church.

In Judaism the practice of continence was encouraged for periods of time, sometimes in connection with cultic occasions (such as the Days of Atonement), or for soldiers in battle, or as a sign of bereavement or fasting. However, lifelong continence—that is, celibacy—was not an acceptable life's choice since all healthy Jewish males were expected to procreate, and

1

2 Celibacy

Jewish law prohibited unmarried Jews from becoming priests. Roman law, also, discouraged celibacy by placing penalites on bachelorhood while rewarding women who gave birth to three or more children.

It is generally accepted that while Jesus remained unmarried, the twelve, including John, were married. Several early Christian writers—among them Origen and Tertullian—made reference to the possibility of Paul, also, being married. Since Paul was a Pharisee, it is unlikely that he deviated from tradition in that important matter.

Continence was not emphasized by Jesus except when he made reference to those who were eunuchs for the sake of the Kingdom (Matt. 19.10-12). Some hold that he was referring to second marriages, but there seems to be no unanimity on that point. (*The Westminster Dictionary of Christian Theology*. Alan Richardson and John Bowden, eds. Philadelphia. The Westminster Press 1981.)

In the early Church, emphasis was placed on abstinence rather than on lifelong celibacy. If the Church concerned itself with sexual practices, it did so within the context of married life, stressing periodic abstinence, rather than celibacy as a permanent way of life. A life of continence was encouraged only after the death of a spouse. Celibacy was not associated with ecclesiastical office, nor did the writers of the Bible make any essential connection between celibacy and the clerical office. Throughout the Hebrew and Christian Scriptures, however, there is concern for the proper use of the sexual function and for the impact that this function has on the larger social structure. Likewise, in religious systems outside of the Judeo-Christian tradition, we find concern for understanding and proper integration of sexual activity within society. There seems to be a universal, tacit awareness that human sexuality is a force to be reckoned with and that there is a corresponding need for it to be brought under the control of social, cultural, and religious value systems. As in the Jewish and Christian traditions, there seems to be an underlying belief that the sexual function has a mysterious, transcendent, almost mystical dimension that needs to be taken seriously.

We need merely cast a casual glance at a daily newspaper, a weekly news magazine, or a nightly TV newscast to become aware of the reality that much of our daily news is concerned with sex in one violent form or another. Likewise, as we watch TV commercials or page through catalogues, we are impressed by the use of sexual attraction as a technique in selling everything from aspirin and automobiles to zippers and zwieback.

There seems to be no end to the dismaying public revelation of our vulnerability and susceptibility to this awesome, wonderful, and, at times, frightening power that is part and parcel of our humanity, that plays such a dramatic role in our relationships with one another.

In the issue of Newsweek dated July 20, 1987, there was an intriguing article on the emergence of groups modeled on AA and other self-help programs but designed for those whose sexual activity has become unmanageable. The participants in these self-help groups are established and well-educated types from many walks of life including politics, business, and even the ministry.

It is with good reason, then, that our social and religious systems have attempted—sometimes with sublime wisdom and at other times with abominable ignorance and prejudice—to help us come to terms and live in some peace with our sexuality.

The Roman Catholic Church is conspicuous for her interest and involvement in the sexual behaviour and attitudes of her members and of society at large. She has consistently maintained a vigorous stand in the areas of birth control, premarital sex, homosexuality, and other sexual behaviour. But, as often as not, her public stance reflects more accurately the subjective biases of the cultural value system of her spokespersons, rather than a truly biblical emphasis on redemption from sin and a concurrent growth into a covenant bonded in divine mercy. The Church's abiding interest and concern are also evident from the fact that she alone, of all Christian denominations of the West, has maintained the institution of a celibate clergy and a form of religious life requiring a vow of celibacy. Lately, however, we note an increase of interest in the practice of celibacy as a way of life in some of the more traditional Protestant denominations, most notably the Anglicans and the Lutherans, as well as in the ecumenical community of Taize in France.

Just as the Church at large is susceptible to the ebb and flow of conventional cultural value systems, including the sexual mores of any given epoch and culture, so too, celibate clerical and religious states absorb and manifest the sexual values of the society in which they are found.

Today we find diocesan ordinaries and superiors of religious men and women, as well as abbots and abbesses of monasteries, who are increasingly preoccupied with the problems of members who suffer from more or less serious psychosexual stresses. Oftentimes those stresses may be acted out in behaviours that are painfully destructive, not only for the individual but for the church community as well. But even when those stresses do not lead to inappropriate external behaviour, they take a tremendous toll in emotional and spiritual suffering.

It is not unusual to awaken in the morning to the news that a revered and respected public person—perhaps a mayor, a teacher or a pastor—has been charged with a public morals offense. More than one Catholic parish community in our country has suffered the trauma of watching a member of its clergy be charged, found guilty, and given a long prison term for child sexual molestation. And of course, there is the ongoing trauma of attempting to deal with the victims of these tragedies.

Are we to become cynical and disenchanted because of deviant sexual behaviour in others, particularly those who have traditionally been the object of unquestioned public trust? Better, let us realize that it is time to become mature and responsible, to let go of childish fantasies in which we project our delusions of total goodness and purity onto objects, institutions, or persons outside of ourselves, only to damn them when they fail to live up to and substantiate our fantasies. We are living in a time when Christian people have a special need to learn the healing value of forgiving and being forgiven.

We must honestly admit that whatever we do, whatever state of life we embrace, the choice comes from within the context of our sinful humanity—sinful, but endowed with a spark of the Divinity that moves us towards the fullness of love. We need to humbly recognize that neither our divine origin nor our destiny to union with all creation in love precludes the actual here-and-now condition of "not being there yet." On the other hand, we should not be deceived into thinking that because we happen to be experiencing the destructive force of sin in our lives, we are excluded from the kingdom that is coming to be, even now, in that sinful condition. When we are able and willing to recognize, admit to, and be responsible for the sin of the world as it exists in us as we wait to be redeemed in our lives and actions, it is then that we are freed from the need to project blame and condemnation on the rapist, the child molester, the unfaithful spouse, or the unfaithful celibate. Then we can recognize a brother or sister in need of healing, understanding, and compassionate forgiveness. "There, but for the grace of God, go I" becomes not just an abstract pietism, but the genuine cry of a compassionate heart, the heart of a person who knows that given the same circumstances, the right combination of deprivation and felt need, with a sufficient amount of motivation and opportunity, any one of us could behave in a similar fashion. Likewise, if we will be honest enough, many of us must admit that our road towards mature and responsible marriage or celibacy has been marked with failures and mistakes. Genuine forgiveness is the fruit of a wise and humble heart that knows its own propensity for sin. But persons who stand in self-righteous horror at the sins and failures of others are beyond forgiveness. They can neither forgive nor be forgiven, for they are blind to an awareness of their own sin that lies, alive and well, within their unconscious from where they project it onto persons and objects safely beyond themselves.

Moreover, it seems to me, we need to forgive ourselves, one another, and the institution we call Mother Church, which, in spite of her accumulated wisdom and holiness, has at times allowed those very virtues to become lost in human ignorance and fear. The currents and tides of history have nudged her away from an identity as a pilgrim church, aware of sinfulness and infidelity but grounded in the hope of the promise of forgiveness. She manifests her susceptibility to fear by a thrust for power and control, combined with an emphasis on conformity to law and order. Her nurturing, life-giving instincts succumb to controlling, inhibiting drives for domination and certitude that are far removed from the experience of the mystery of God, for which the human heart longs.

Probably it is accurate to say that many of us of the over-forty generation have a considerable amount of prejudicial baggage to let go of before we can seriously consider chastity a relevant and positive factor in our sexual relationships. Too often in the past—as, unfortunately, even today in many quarters—sexual feelings were seen as the first step towards mortal sin. Therefore, anything remotely connected with any person, occasion, or object that stimulated sexual responses was to be avoided at all costs. By implication, the related thoughts and feelings, as well, were seen as dangerous. Since those thoughts and desires arose unbidden from some mysterious place in our consciousness, the result was that even our feelings and fantasies became an imagined occasion of sin. That led not only to a general feeling of guilt and anxiety over questions of our own goodness but, sometimes, to a complete suppression of feelings, desires, and fantasies. The consequent self-deception of thinking that the "devil" had been tamed by this suppression was often as ruinous as the guilt and anxiety caused in the first place by the troublesome thoughts and desires. In fact, the so-called devil had merely gone undergound and changed his face, only to reappear in any number of guises, such as projection, self-righteousness, emotional paralysis, and a variety of sexual malfunctions that surfaced later in life.

If we place celibacy and chastity in their proper perspective and relationship to one another, we can see how those virtues help us in our search for spiritual and psychological integrity.

St. Thomas Aquinas treats chastity (Summa Q. 151—"Of Chastity") as a virtue that is a norm for all Christians. In more recent times, chastity has become identified in the popular mind with the vow taken by religious men and women who are required to remain celibate. To remain chaste has, therefore, mistakenly come to mean being sexually inactive. Added to this misunderstanding was the erosion of our positive attitudes towards sexuality by the influence of Platonic duality that crept into early Christian thinking about matter, spirit, and the notion of sin. As a result of the Platonic influence, Christianity was pervaded by a general mistrust of anything that had to do with the body and its feeling functions, particularly in the area of sexuality. The early ascetics of the desert were clearly influenced by that kind of thinking, and the works of Augustine show similar strains of Platonism.

Around the third and fourth centuries there began to appear Christian writings that said marriage is good, but celibacy is better. It is possible that as Christianity spread more and more into the pagan world, the link between ritual impurity and sacrifice affected Christian thinking. Obviously, it seems that pagan cultic superstitions had something to do with the custom of priests abstaining from sexual intercourse on the night prior to their celebration of the Eucharist. At the end of the fourth century, that custom was formalized into a law requiring abstinence of married priests when they were going to celebrate Mass. So it was until the end of the twelfth century.

In the interim, celibacy began to emerge as a means of making the law of abstinence effective. The Council of Nicaea (A.D. 325) chose not to make celibacy obligatory among clerics while praising it for those holding higher office. At about the same time, the Eastern Church began to choose its bishops from among celibate monks. In the sixth century, the Emperor Justinian decreed that a person who had children could not be a bishop and that a married cleric must abstain from sexual relations with his wife. The main reason for that was not spiritual but economic, for it had become necessary to find a way to stop the flow of Church property into the families of priests.

In the seventh century, at the Council of Trullo, the Eastern Church made a definite law about celibacy for higher clergy but, in the West, actual laws of celibacy prior to ordination came about only in the twelfth century. In 1139 Pope Alexander II, at the Second Lateran Council, decreed that marriages of clergy after ordination are invalid. Two succeeding Popes, Alexander III and Celestine II, reaffirmed that decree in 1180 and 1198, respectively. Until the end of the fifteenth century, both clergy and laity reacted negatively to the law and it was almost universally scorned. By that time, pagan cultic superstition had declined as the major issue, but child inheritance and nepotism had become a major problem which, theoretically, a celibate clergy would help overcome. Finally, in the seventeenth century, with the establishment of seminaries for the formation of clergy, celibacy was firmly established as a requirement for all clergy of the Roman rite. (Cf. Schillebeeckx, Edward. Ministry: Leadership in the Community of Jesus Christ. New York: Crossroads 1981.)

It is important to keep in mind that while political and socioeconomic influences seem to have been determining factors in the emergence of celibacy as a norm for all clergy, priests in increasing numbers had been practicing celibacy by free choice since the fourth century. That was done after the example of Christ himself, as well as the example of the monks who practiced celibacy as a substitute for martyrdom which had ceased to be the norm.

Today, although we have progressed beyond the pagan notion of cultic purity, negative attitudes towards the body and its functions continue to plague us and tarnish our understanding of and relationship with the physical aspects of our being. Remnants of Jansenism and Puritanism continue to cast suspicion on pleasures of the body; thus, all too many of us are uncomfortable with pleasures related to our sensible appetites. Such negative and suspicious attitudes manifest themselves today in the form of religious fundamentalism, both within and without the Catholic Church. Within the Church, many movements that have demonstrated an unbalanced and sordid preoccupation with sexuality and sexual behaviour, almost to the exclusion of all other Christian values, stem from an alienation from material things that is rooted in Platonic duality. This dualism has almost fatally flawed our understanding of the Virginity of Mary and, through the centuries, has caused her name to be invoked as the patroness of negative movements which impugn the dignity of sexuality and sexual relationships. Conversely, the hedonistic compulsion for pleasure, the sexual freedom advocated in many quarters, and the widespread cynicism and disdain for any sexual restraints whatever are but other aspects of the same Platonic dualism.

A reflective look at some of our traditional values may reveal wisdom that will enable us to achieve a balance in the midst of so much excess. According to St. Thomas, reaching a balance is what chastity is all about.

Chastity takes its name from chastise, which means to cleanse, purify, and moderate our sense appetites. In its most true meaning, chastise does not mean to punish; it means to guide and discipline the sense appetites towards a proper and harmonious relationship with the reason and the will. Far from being a negative element, chastity is positive in that it brings about balance. It purifies our sense appetites from selfishness, but does not attempt to eliminate them altogether. Thus chastity, as it has come to be associated almost exclusively with sexual appetite, is the virtue that moderates use of the sexual function in accord with the rational discernment of what is right and proper in any set of circumstances.

To be chaste means to place one's sexuality and sexual appetites within proper relationship to one's other appetites, reason, and will. In order to achieve that, one must take into account not only the well-being and needs of oneself and one's sexual partner, but also the overall good of society. Sexuality, according to this norm, is not one's private domain with personal prerogatives over which one has immediate and unquestioned authority; it must always be integrated into the larger social reality. Indeed, if sexuality can be seen as a process by which each of us is integrated into the social environment, then chastity is the virtue which guides the integrating process.

Chastity, then, is not the nonuse of one's sexual faculties; rather, it is intelligent and compassionate interaction with another; it is self-giving as well as receiving. Properly understood, chastity is the virtue that makes sexuality humanizing and fulfilling for all concerned. It enhances male-female relationships by elevating them to their full dignity. Chastity enables us to recognize our selfishness and our propensity to manipulate and exploit relationships for our own gain, and helps us place those tendencies in proper perspective as we see them for what they are. Chastity sensitizes us to our interrelatedness with other persons, each of whom has a unique constellation of needs and feelings. Chastity gives a perspective from which to make decisions and to get beyond our egotistical narrowness to a mutually life-giving relationship with the world around us.

Using St. Thomas' criteria, we see that attitudes explicit or implied, attitudes on the part of Church, society, or culture that tend to discourage male-female interaction in order to avoid sexual feelings under the pretext of protecting the virtue of chastity are, in fact, contrary to that virtue. Practices or attitudes that interfere with positive, constructive relationships between men and women, either celibate or married, seem to be contrary to the highest meaning of the virtue. Being the virtue that enhances and ennobles male-female relationships and, ultimately, all human relationships, chastity becomes a force for bringing about community. In chastity we become mindful of the rights and needs of others, rather than exploit them for our own gain or personal pleasure.

The virtue of chastity provides a measure whereby we judge all of our attitudes and relationships. Chastity is to be seen as regulating not only genital-sexual relationships, but the entire spectrum of male-female interactions, ultimately reaching beyond the intimacy of the home into society at large.

This virtue can be understood as the ground on which we seek to build a community out of right relationships, with each person's dignity and well-being of primary value. Gender and sexual function are not the exclusive criteria by which one person is related to another in friendship, in marriage, or in the larger community; rather, one's giftedness and dignity as a child of God are the primary measures of one's place and function in all human relationships.

Chastity can also be understood as the foundational virtue that provides a standard by which we can evaluate and give perspective to the tradition of celibacy in the Church. Rather than trying to understand chastity from the point of view of celibacy, we need to turn the process around and measure celibacy from the perspective of chastity. Similarly, rather than evaluating and guiding relationships from the perspective of celibacy, saying that not having sexual relationships is better than having them and that having less sex is better than more, we can evaluate marriage, also, from the point of view of chastity. We will then be able to see chastity as the virtue that brings both celibates and married couples into mutually affirmative relationships.

Courageous honesty may require some painful growth in our understanding of chastity and celibacy. It may also require the leaving behind of
some cherished beliefs and assumptions but, ultimately, honesty will lead
us to a clearer understanding of what it means to be a celibate growing into
deeper and more lifegiving relationships.

St. Thomas Aquinas has made some intersting observations under the
heading of virginity (Q. 152; Art. 2: Is Virginity Lawful?). He begins by
questioning the lawfulness of virginity (celibacy) as a lifelong choice,
wondering if one has the right to refrain altogether from sexual relations.
He suggests that total abstinence may be in violation of the natural precept
to procreate and participate in the preservation of the species (Gen. 1:27-
28). Likewise, he observes that since all virtue is essentially a matter of
balance—a moderate use rather than a nonuse of the sense appetites—
chastity is the proper use of the sexual function in moderation; total
abstinence, then, may be a violation of that virtue because it is extreme—
not moderate, not virtuous. In some cultures, continence has been a
punishable crime. Plato himself offered sacrifice in an attempt to atone for
his lifelong celibacy. The point being made is that we have no right to
lightly dispense ourselves from the natural precept of procreation.

Thomas resolves the dilemma by concluding that virginity and celibacy
may be good, but, he says, they are good only when and insofar as they
enable the persons espousing them to achieve a greater good for society
than they could achieve by marrying.

This greater good is attained by the celibate when his or her life brings
about the spiritual progress of society through contemplation and the fruits
that accrue from that activity. We cannot leave a void; if we dispense ourselves from the primary precept of preserving and advancing the human
species physically, we take upon ourselves the obligation of spiritual generation through a life of contemplation and a sharing of the fruits of that
contemplation for the good of the Church.

Celibacy as a state of life affords the community a visible sign of the
evolution of human relationships towards their perfection in Christlike
love, love that is totally free and self-giving. That is the natural destiny of

all human love. It is the love of Christ made manifest in his body, the Church. Celibacy is the foreshadowing sign pointing to the realization of that destiny from within the here-and-now community made up of persons who are "not there yet." Such a possibility can be fully grasped only if the community is composed of married and celibate people together. Either group, without the presence and influence of the other, can too easily become lost in its own limited perspective. The celibate can too easily forget that the perfection of human love happens within the struggle and pain of human relationships: of feeling not fully understood or of being unable to fully understand; of having to stretch past one's frailty so as to forgive, even while not receiving full forgiveness; of being called upon to give and give again, even when giving is taken too much for granted.

On the other hand, the married person may easily forget that human love can never be fully contained or realized, even in the ecstasy of sexual union and the procreation of one's own kind. The human heart is open to infinity, to God. Nothing less can ever satisfy it. Even when our human love is as good as it can be, we experience—at times, acutely—a longing of the heart for more. There is a point of inner solitude that aches for the One who can fill it and quiet its yearning. That solitary ache can drive us to a restless search in the deluded hope that the longing can be put to rest by the perfect lover, the idealized hero or heroine. It is then we need to be reminded that that solitude, that hunger is not the terminal point of love but only its beginning. Through that point, when we are ready and willing to embrace it, we become one with the self-giving love of Christ, who gave all and expected nothing in return; who served, even while others were plotting against him; who forgave everyone, even as some were jeering; and who, by embracing the mystery of his life and death, passed into the fullness of all life with the Creator. It is by entering into that point of solitude and resting in it that we are able to pass through it in order to enter into human relationships free from unrealistic expectations and demands.

The paradoxical situation of the human person is dramatically addressed for us in the story of the encounter of Jesus with the Samaritan woman at the well (Jn. 4. 7- 26). The woman, who had been searching for happiness in a succession of husbands, was effectively drawn by Jesus to the realization that her search should begin and end within her own life, entered into and lived in union with God's Word. In him, we are drawn to a unity with, and an acceptance of, ourselves. He is the one who unmasks the deception of thinking that happiness and fulfillment lie outside of ourselves, in other persons or in things. As we enter into and embrace our own solitude, we pass through it into relationships that are free from the entanglements of our egotistical expectations and needs. Celibacy, like marriage, can find its life only in the center of our personal solitude.

Celibacy may be seen as a two-edged sword that will either help us to move deeper into the mystery of human relationships or, failing that, cause us to live in the egotistical shallows of personal development; it will admit of no middle way. Growth can happen only when the challenge of celibacy is accepted and responded to personally in every aspect of one's life and relationships; that challenge cannot live when it is passively offered or accepted as a by-product of the clerical or religious state. The very essence of personal growth and development lies, first of all, in the ability to choose and, beyond that, in a willingness to make choices—to actively make choices and accept responsibility for the consequences of those choices, as opposed to passively allowing our lives to be led by circumstance. It is the movement that finally separates us from dependency on our parent figures and takes us into the role of becoming our own parent, so that we allow our lives to flow from the center of our existence into mature ownership of and responsibility for our choices.

I am reminded of the marvelous story of Samuel in the temple of the Lord (1 Samuel 3). Samuel was the child given by God to Hannah in response to her prayers. After he had been weaned she took him to the temple at Shilo and placed him under the care of Eli the priest (1 Samuel 1:27-28). Samuel was in the temple to serve the Lord. "For his whole life he will be given over to the Lord" (1 Samuel 1:28), because of a decision made by his mother and ratified by another, Eli the priest of the Lord.

In the routine service of the temple under the watchful eye of Eli, young Samuel grew to maturity. The story of Samuel's call is familiar to most. Old Eli was asleep in his quarters. Samuel was lying down in the temple where the Ark of the Covenant was kept. Twice Samuel heard the voice of the Lord calling him and twice Samuel, quite understandably, reported to Eli thinking that it was he who had called. Twice Eli, equally mystified, sent Samuel back to his quarters. The third time however, the wise old man realized that Samuel was being called by the Lord and told him to return to await the Lord's call again. It is at this point that we have that marvelous and touching encounter between the Lord and his servant Samuel. "The Lord came and stood there, calling as at the other times, '"Samuel! Samuel!"' Then Samuel said, '"speak, for your servant is listening."'

In this modest little story we have the unfolding of a young, immature soul into a fully mature relationship with God. Personal, intimate, life-giving, not only for Samuel but for Eli and the people of Israel as well. In this event Samuel grew from a boy whose life was circumscribed by the decisions of others, his mother's, Eli's and by the duties of the temple, to a young man, fully self possessed, an adult ready to hear and to respond to his own call in freedom. He was no longer in the temple serving the Lord because of a decision made by others, nor was his life simply circumscribed by the daily routine of a temple functionary. He was a prophet—called, anointed, and sent with power to be God's Word to His people.

We cannot fully assess or appreciate the meaning of this event for Samuel unless we likewise understand Eli's essential role. If Samuel was able to recognize and respond to the voice of God calling him, it was because of Eli's wisdom. This event in the life of Eli and Samuel is really the story of a spiritual parent or guide recognizing and accepting a moment in which a student or child is called to maturity and autonomy. It is a moment of crisis for both. The young person must bravely reach out into the darkness of personal autonomy and responsible freedom; the guide and teacher must courageously and humbly turn loose of parental authority and control allowing the young person to get about the task of responsible participation in the life of the community. Up until now young Samuel "did not yet know the Lord: the Word of the Lord had not yet been revealed to him." (1Samuel 3:7). It was when Eli knew that the Lord was now speaking directly to Samuel, and sent him away from himself to hear the Lord directly, that Samuel entered into his manhood, no longer a disciple, a temple orderly, but now one who had received and made his own the Word of the Lord. He appropriated and interiorized what previously had been passively accepted through the decisions of others. And the power of God's Word was manifest in his life.

It was Eli's paternal love and holy wisdom that enabled him to recognize this moment of Samuel's emancipation from his own authority of mediation into adulthood and a free response to God's call.

The implications are clear and inescapable for church as mother and teacher, for religious communities and seminaries as well as spiritual directors charged with the formation of the young for prophetic ministry. Quite simply, the major task is to instruct and lead them in the art of contemplative attentiveness to God's Word being addressed to them, discerning with them God's call emerging as their lives encounter and respond to the demands of mature growth and development, letting go of authoritative control, releasing them into the prophetic service of God's eternal Word.

On the other hand, individuals, celibate as well as married, have a model by which to examine their response to actualize God's call and step out in bold and prophetic living. The unfortunate alternative, which appears all too common today, not only for religious and priests, but the People of God as well, is to continue our entire lives passively accepting a role of perpetual dependency, never fully stepping into a mature, responsible, adult relationship with a god who calls us to go where we ourselves would not choose to go, to do that which we ourselves would not choose to do. This is the ground out of which any true evangelical obedience must grow and bear fruit. Likewise, the void left by celibacy will not be quietened by anything less than being the space wherein one encounters the living God of eternal promise and possibility.

To recapture celibacy as a valid, positive presence in the Church and society, we need to put into perspective the historical and socioeconomic factors that contributed to its being drawn into the legal, bureaucratic structure of the Church. Celibacy first emerged in Christian consciousness as a freely chosen way to express the single-minded pursuit of the Christian mystery. The fact that it has subsequently been drawn into a legal and oftentimes legalistic framework does not detract from its value and potential fruitfulness as a freely chosen way to manifest evangelical values. But if celibacy is to fully realize its potential for fruitfulness in the community, the obligation must be interiorized and owned as a personal choice.

At Vatican Council II the Fathers testified to a desire to see celibacy returned to its true meaning as a witness to Gospel values, a sign of the Kingdom. That new impetus encourages celibate persons to reassess the quality of their celibate state and their commitment to embody the contemplative, mystical, and prophetic dimension of the charism, as opposed to simply living as conventional, institutional functionaries. Likewise, it challenges Church bureaucracy to examine its own values and attitudes towards the legal control and bureaucratic pragmatism that underlies much of the Church's official position towards celibates and the charism of celibacy.

2

Celibacy as a Living Presence in Society

A commitment to celibacy is a radical position for a person or an organization to take. To deliberately make such a commitment is to make a remarkably bold statement about the strength of one's convictions. Similarly, when an institution deems its message or statement about the human condition and its mission to society so important that at least some of its members refrain from marriage and the generation of physical life, there is certainly reason to pause and listen to the message conveyed by such extraordinary action. No matter what our beliefs or the motives that drive us in life, when we, as members of a society, are confronted by a group of people who have taken a position that dramatically deviates from the norm, we are stopped short by a forceful message that far exceeds the power of any theological argument.

When we lose sight of the radical nature of celibacy, when it becomes just another piece of conventional religious paraphernalia, then its value and its intended statement, along with the credibility of persons and institutions espousing it, are eroded to a point where it may become counterproductive or, at least, irrelevant. The religious state and the celibate person lose their priestly and prophetic potential when celibacy, as a living and dynamic presence, loses its ability to confront and challenge human consciousness and the assumptions that hold it in bondage.

One result of the institutionalization of celibacy is that celibate individuals themselves may never grasp the significance of their own identity and role in modern society. The celibate person's role extends beyond the boundaries of self into the larger church community and even into secular society. If the celibate person is, in his or her own consciousness, no different in perceptions, visions, and values than the society in which he or she is called to live, then celibacy is not only a folly to the members of that society but a puzzle and a mystifying burden to the celibate person as well. Instead of being integrated with personal identity so as to be a source of energy, an ally in one's ministry, a personal and communal statement to the world, celibacy becomes an enervating burden, a source of stress in an already stressful world.

Celibacy that is effective finds its roots in the chaste celibacy of Jesus Christ, whose identity, in turn, was rooted in his unity with God. Any attempt to understand the source of living celibacy inevitably takes us in that direction. If we are to live celibacy positively—indeed, chastely—our lives will necessarily move beyond mere theological assent and conformity to culturally and historically conditioned circumstances into personal, transforming relationships with the living Christ. To take celibacy as a way of life—either voluntarily, as in religious life, or as a condition imposed as a requirement for ordination—is to accept the Word of God, Jesus Christ, as the model for our lives and mission. That acceptance must ultimately allow the reality of celibacy to penetrate to the center of our lives and to remain there as a sign of a personal and free choice, continuing the process of surrender to the mystery of God; otherwise, the reality will eventually dry up and become no more than an empty shell of what once was—or could have been—a living statement of our desire to be given over to the mystery of God's love for creation.

To freely and knowingly embrace celibacy as a way of life or to have celibacy imposed as a requirement for Holy Orders, as in the Western Catholic Church, is to center our lives in a reality that transcends conventional, everyday consciousness and understanding of contemporary society. It is to make a statement of our faith and belief that in its ongoing development, human consciousness is open to a love that transcends family, race, and nation and reaches out to embrace all humankind.

Far from being a mere bureaucratic organization, a network of laws imposing an external identity and code of behaviour, Christianity is primarily an inner force which, when released, moves our relationships beyond all boundaries of political, racial, sexual, economic, and social distinctions into a radical unity in the life of the One who is the source of all that exists and who draws all into unity (Gal. 3.26-29). Christianity calls equally to all of humanity to become one in the fullness of God, even as we live in our time and place, struggling in the poverty of our present relationships. Christianity is not only, or even primarily, a religious system of theological belief; it is essentially a force that is capable of transforming human consciousness and, ultimately, the course of history. Men and women who choose celibacy as a way of living in the world accept the challenge of opening themselves to living on the forward edge of this force.

I do not mean to say that the celibate is in some way favored with superior consciousness or virtue. It would be just as foolish to say that all married persons, because they witness to the possibility and promise of married love, actually now enjoy and experience the fullness of the perfection of the sacrament of matrimony. In fact, long marriages are as inspirational and wonderful as they are because the partners carry with them patience, compassion, gentleness, and understanding that have been won through long years of failure, dissapointment, sin, and repentance. Similarly, the celibate is one who witnesses out of his or her struggles with failure, misunderstanding, sin, and forgiveness. Just as in marriage, so in the celibate state, we all mean to say that, somehow, the reality of the Kingdom is being made manifest through the here-and-now condition of our humanity. The Kingdom is created out of our human struggles. The qualities of peace and patience that are the fruits of our struggles in faith reach beyond our own experience and touch deeply the lives of those around us in a more powerful way than do theological exhortations.

Sooner or later, every celibate person needs to face the reality that celibacy cannot be entered into or sustained on a rational theological level, nor can it be sustained simply because it happens to be a matter of law or a secondary consequence stemming from the choice of a state of life. The cost of not facing this reality honestly and courageously can be heavy. Celibacy cannot live when it is rooted only in conformity to convention, even religious convention. Certainly it often begins there, but a commitment to celibacy is one that ultimately must be dealt with on a level of faith that is rooted in a personal and ongoing relationship with a god who is the God of life. This god is constantly self-revealing in life, and we have been created to share the ongoing divine self-revelation in the quality of our lives and relationships.

The price for not sustaining celibacy as a living and dynamic force in our lives is that celibacy itself can become a source of death to our spirits. It will either live and manifest itself in bold and enthusiastic engagement in the adventure of life or it will die. Again, there is no middle ground. If it dies, much dies with it. Here I am not speaking of the state of individuals who have seen fit to move from celibacy to marriage. Indeed, they may have done the more creative and positive thing in comparison with others who have abandoned celibacy but have kept the mantle of external appearance while having long since allowed the living spirit of celibacy to wither away. I am speaking—but not exclusively—of those who enter into temporary or habitual illicit liasons. There are others whose lives have dried up in eccentric, self-indulgent behaviour, whose interpersonal relationships are brusque, distant or indifferent, perhaps openly hostile; they are just as guilty of sin against their sexuality, just as much in violation of the virtue of chastity, as are those who experience more dramatic and explicit external failures.

In the fifth chapter of the Acts of the Apostles, we find a rather startling and dramatic image of what happens when someone attempts to play "approach-avoidance" with his or her offering of self to God. "There was another man, however, called Ananias. He and his wife, Sapphira, agreed to sell a property; but with his wife's connivance he kept back part of the proceeds, and brought the rest and presented it to the apostles" (Acts 5.1-2). When he was confronted by the apostle Peter, "Ananias fell down dead. This made a profound impression on everyone present" (Acts 5.5). As the story develops, we read that the wife of Ananias pays the same price for her complicity (Acts 5.10). We can too readily pass over this incident and dismiss it as being just another instance of biblical drama intended to intimidate and coerce less sophisticated souls. In fact, the incident is rather remarkable in its insight into psychological realities and the price we pay for attempting to "lie to the Holy Spirit" (Acts 5.3). Peter had admonished Ananias by reminding him that it was not to men that he had lied, but to God (Acts 5.4). The truth being illustrated is just as relevant today as it was then and the consequences just as dire, although perhaps not as immediately apparent.

Our human nature, created out of God's eternal truth, reflects that truth and is destined to live in the eternal glory of that truth, which is love. Jesus Christ is the final revelation of that truth. To open ourselves to a relationship with him is to assent to living in the unfolding of our own truth. We cannot give ourselves half way, any more than we can go only half way in marriage. For any relationship to live, it must be open to growth and movement beyond the narrow boundaries of the individual ego to a oneness in mutuality. In a relationship of mutuality—when egocentric fears have been surrendered and one is able to be truly present to another—a glimpse of true freedom is had and the richness of true relationship is experienced. In the celibate state, to stop short of total self-giving and total surrender to the mystery of our own becoming is to die spiritually. It is an attempt to live a lie, not a lie of the mind and the lips, but a lie from the center of the heart. If celibacy has become a land of the living dead for many, it is because we have thought we could have it both ways: going through the motions of giving while protecting our own preserves of power, control, material security, worldly esteem, and the rest.

We are in fact lying to ourselves as well as to God. It is the ultimate lie, not a lie of the lips, but of the heart, a lie to the Holy Spirit living within us.

Unless the celibate's life is grounded in a basic relationship with God, that life is doomed to frustration, tension, anxiety, and, ultimately, to an experience of futility and emptiness. The individual who has not based the celibate option on a personal, ongoing relationship with God will be deprived not only of the legitimate pleasures and satisfactions of married life and love, but also will not have satisfied a deeper, authentic need for creative, life-giving engagement in the life and ministry of the Church. Celibacy will not be perceived or experienced as a positive force, generating life and proclaiming the presence and possibility of creative options in Christianity. Rather than being a voluntary self-surrender into participation in the eternal mystery of God, revealed in Jesus Christ, celibacy will be experienced and perceived as an illogical, perplexing, even a maddening deprivation of legitimate human satisfactions.

The Church came into being because Jesus Christ entered into individual relationships and called into his discipleship persons having names, dreams, hopes, needs, and relationships. Those persons were much like you and me, with lives marked by some successes as well as some failures. They were trying to discover what life in general—and theirs in particular—was all about. Their personal relationships with Christ became part of the overall picture, yet he added a new dimension through a creative process that led to purification of the popular concept of the meaning of life. As that creative process continued, a transformation took place, opening the disciples to a deeper union with Jesus, enabling him to lead them to the Cross and to the total dismantling of everything they believed about themselves and their place in the world, of who Jesus was and what he was going to do for them. That dismantling and emptying process was so complete that as Jesus died in truth, they entered into the process of dying to all that was not true, to all that was phony and superficial in their lives.

If we look closely at the relationship between Jesus and his disciples, we will see that it drew them away from illusions about reality and their perceptions of who Jesus was, and toward a more fundamental truth. They were purified of the narrowness of their expectations and their perceived needs and led into the truth of Christ on the cross. Jesus' love for his disciples would not allow him to be anything but true to his own mission. In pursuing his own truth, Christ revealed to the disciples a truth about themselves of which they were unaware. And they would have remained unaware had Jesus not revealed, through his life and relationships, their true potential for love and generous service.

The Church of the Resurrection is a church that was poured out through the death of Jesus, but we oftentimes forget that it took root in a community of people who had been prepared by being dismantled and emptied, purified from their delusions. In short, they were made broken-hearted in order to be ready to receive the inpouring of the Holy Spirit. Just as Jesus passed out of his body into the full life of God, the Christ-event entered into and became incarnate in the Mystical Body of Christ, the Church. By way of personal, purifying, transforming relationships, a life of union with God through Jesus Christ became the norm for the Pentecost community and succeeding generations of Christians for the first several hundred years, as well as for the mystics and saints of the Church right down to our own time. What the saints, contemplatives, and mystics of our time have experienced was the norm for the early Christians and should be the norm for all of us. The Church is not, never was, and never can be simply a matter of orthodoxy, ritual, and formula. Before all else, the Church must lead each of us to a personal, purifying, and transforming relationship with God that begins in this life and becomes an ongoing union with him, continuing throughout eternity.

The disciples, and the first post-Resurrection Christians as well, experienced in their relationship to Jesus, the Christ, risen from the dead, an opening to and an actualization of new possibilities in their lives—possibilities and empowerment previously hidden from conscious awareness. Hence, the primitive Church was characterized by the release of a desire, even an impatience, to leave behind past ways that had seemed so logical and normal. Conventional value systems and the accepted wisdom of the time no longer could contain or define the lives and actions of the early

Christians. Thenceforth, there would be a whole new reality of promise and possibility that could never have come to those people had they not been in that first purifying and dismantling relationship with Jesus. Thus, a fundamental principle of Christian life was revealed.

Simply put, the Christian community is essentially the medium that conveys and imparts an experience of a relationship to the Risen Christ as personal saviour. It is Christ-centered in that each person's life is opened to a personal and unique relationship with Jesus, the Christ. Even now, that relationship continues to purify, transform, and empty us as it leads us to readiness for union with God. Such readiness includes an awakening of our consciousness to a realization of heretofore unrecognized potentialities within ourselves, as well as within humanity in general. A genuine, living relationship with Christ leads us into the mystery and wonder of the depths of potential in our own lives. As a personal saviour, Jesus is the one who introduces me to myself at a deep level that I had never been aware of. I encounter the Christ-event in the depths of my own self. At that level I enter into a union with God that enables divine self-revelation to continue through my existence in human relationships. God's being, in love, becomes incarnate in my flesh. Likewise the Church, a living community of people, lives out the same mystery of purification, transformation, and union.

The early Church community was essentially one in which people received guidance, encouragement, and support, as well as instruction, so that they could come to know—that is, experience—Jesus Christ as personal saviour. The community served to teach and to form the uninitiated in preparation for entrance into that personal and transforming relationship with the living Christ. Theology was never seen as a substitute for a personal experience of a living, dynamic, and transforming reality. The process of coming to know Jesus Christ—first through experience and then through a personal, ongoing, creative relationship—was the norm of Christianity for the first fifteen centuries, right up to the Middle Ages. Accordingly, the expectation was that the normal fruit of prayer, study of Sacred Scripture, and celebration of the sacraments would be growth into a personal, transforming relationship that would enable the individual Christian to live a life of union with God.

As the age of martyrdom gave way to the age of the desert ascetics, the same process continued, always with the expectation that the participants would be drawn into a personal relationship of purification and transformation. When the early ascetics studied Scripture, they did so with the intention of interiorizing the Word in such a way that they lived the Word and the Word lived in them, transforming them and their relationships. As monasticism developed over the centuries, the monks came to an understanding of the whole process by which that transformation occurred; they systematized it in order that it could be taught to others.

The system was made up of three distinct phases. The first phase, the attentive reading of Sacred Scripture, known as lectio, is a listening kind of reading that patiently waits in trust for the Word to reveal its own mystery. It is a recognition that the mystery of the revealed Word cannot be contained within the limits of mere understanding because it has life and meaning that transcends human logic (Heb. 4.12- 13). After reading, the monks pondered, ruminating what they had read in an attempt to allow the mystery of the Word to encounter the mystery and perplexity, as well as the reality and the promise of their lives. This second phase, known as meditatio, was a quiet savoring of the Word, pondered in expectation. While there was some intellectual involvement and activity, it was characterized by a humble acknowledgement that the Word had its own mystery to reveal. In the third phase, quiet listening and attentiveness to the personal lesson led to an act that came from the heart in a prayer response called oratio. That prayer of the heart was unique, personal, and spontaneous, specific to the experience of encountering God in the Word from within the experience of daily living.

The natural course of the process led to a state of repose and silence in which the monks were united to God in his Living Word at the depths of the soul (Heb. 4.12-13). That experience of a personal and intimate encounter with God was called contemplatio. Rather than being considered an unusual or exceptional phenomenon, it was regarded as the normal fruit of devoted and faithful practice of lectio, meditatio, and oratio. The expectation was that devotion to prayer would lead anyone to personal union with God through an awakening to the Christ-life within. Thus, the contemplative state was the normal condition of a soul given to prayer and the study of the Word. The monk epitomized the vocation of all Christians to become one with the Word of God and to enter into prayer as the way to a personal and living union with God that leads beyond all forms and rites.

Through a prayerful and attentive presence to the Word of God, the monk was called to be a "mother" of the Word. That concept is one of the underlying dynamics of the widespread devotion to Mary that is found throughout both Eastern and Western monasticism. Mary is the model of all Christian prayer because her life was one of openness to the will of God, through which the Word took flesh and entered as one of us into the current of human history, turning it onto another course. It is through devotion and fidelity to reading Sacred Scripture (lectio), meditating on its personal meaning to us within the lived experience of our lives (meditatio), responding to the Word from the center of our hearts (oratio), and being drawn into a personal union with the living God (contemplatio) that we, too, become filled with the life of God, giving it flesh and presence in our lives and relationships.

The Council of Trent (1545 - 1563) marked a dramatic turning point in the life and self-understanding of the Church. That Council was instrumental in reinforcing a drift towards an emphasis on orthodoxy and conformity to external conventions and away from more personal expressions of faith. The Council's emphasis on uniformity was applied to theology and liturgy, as well as to styles of prayer and public devotion. Thus, the mystical and charismatic aspects of Christian faith and practice gave way to the tidiness of law and uniformity in public worship, and personal insights into Sacred Scripture gave way to official interpretation. Gradually, the Pope and, under his authority, the bishops also began to see themselves as custodians of orthodoxy in belief and practice and as administrators of a bureaucracy guarding right order through hierarchical authority. Along with discouraging individual experience in the areas of prayer and devotion, they opposed plurality of forms of worship and liturgy in favor of conformity to the Roman way.

Because of that shift in self-perception on the part of the Church, as well as a variety of other historical and cultural factors, the rest of the sixteenth century continued to see a drifting away from contemplative prayer as a norm for Christians. The faithful were encouraged only to "say their prayers." Studying and praying Sacred Scripture became an exercise of discursive meditation, with emphasis on rational analysis and understanding. The intuitive and affective faculties were left completely out of the prayer experience. Knowing as experience degenerated to mere analytical understanding. The mystery of God, present in his Living Word, became the object of an intellectual exercise that sought to reduce everything to the limits of human intellect.

Eventually, prayer became limited to a ritualistic performance of actions in which the form and the method were more important than the effect they had on individual lives. The doing became more important than the fruit of the doing. A personal, transforming relationship with Christ was replaced by an orthodoxy of theological belief. Personal conversion and inner transformation gave way to emphasis on behaviour according to conventions of decorum and culture. Salvation was equated with the integrity and orthodoxy of one's theology. Virtue was, as often as not, only a successful attempt at suppressing elements of one's behavior or personality that could get one into trouble.

In seminaries and houses of religious formation, emphasis was placed on the proper performance of prescribed prayers and rituals, observance of custom, and external decorum. Life and relationships were kept tidy by emphasis on strict adherence to "the rule," which was guaranteed to lead one to sanctity. In the area of prayer, candidates were trained and encouraged in a variety of "devotions" and the acquisition of indulgences. Lectio was reduced to the reading of the lives of saints, founders, and other inspirational persons. Meditation became simply an intellectual struggle to understand the meaning of a preassigned passage of Scripture, or, as often as not, the reading of someone else's official interpretation of Scripture. Great attention was paid to the obligation of completing certain prescribed formulas and to the dire consequences of neglecting that obligation.

In seminaries, young men were selected on the basis of their intellectual prowess and measured according to their capacity to master the correct theological formulas—in Latin, of course. The idea that one should aspire to a personal union with God through contemplative prayer was looked on with suspicion and actively discouraged. Great value was placed on one's willingness and ability to perform the liturgical services with precision. In so-called contemplative monasteries and convents, work in one form or another was valued above silence and solitude so that, even in those places, a true contemplative was hard to find.

To put it crudely, religious formation became a process similar to that used in military boot camps; candidates were whipped into shape and provided with the necessary academic, professional, and behavioural skills to effectively promote and transmit a belief system that had been reduced to formulas containing dogmatic truths, rituals, and laws. With very few exceptions, the charismatic, contemplative elements of Christianity were almost totally taken over by the legal and bureaucratic elements. Faith was no longer a personal relationship, but conscientious adherence to a codified belief system. Needless to say, celibacy took its lumps as the charismatic, contemplative aspect of the Church succumbed to the power and control of a legal bureaucracy armed with the awesome power to dispatch souls to heaven or to hell, depending on the quality of one's obedience and adherence to the will and whim of hierarchical authorities.

Although legal bureaucracy may have its place, ultimately there must come a point in the spiritual journey where a personal decision is necessary, and the following of Christ—in all its varied forms and manifestations—becomes a personal, unique enterprise within a community of believers. In the process, celibacy is a symbol that signifies a personal, inner vision, a living hope of fulfillment of the promise in our lives.

The questions we need to address most specifically deal with how to respond when a monolithic, authoritarian, and at times unfeeling institution requires, universally, a commitment to celibacy on the part of all who seek ordination. Even though celibacy involves a radical and dramatic public stand against the tide of cultural conventions and values, the Church appropriates the legal authority to impose that condition on those choosing

Holy Orders. The authority of law, however, while possessing the power to require the condition of celibacy, does not possess the power to make celibacy effective, true, or right for every person whom she requires to be celibate. Even in the case of those for whom this state of life may be true and right, once the person has embraced the law, that law—in itself—becomes immaterial and irrelevant simply because it can never transcend the externals of human behaviour. The law of the Church can only provide a kind of external stability, creating an environment wherein one may discover the law that is written on the flesh of one's own heart. As often as not, that is the point at which the celibate option breaks down. We fail to make the leap from legal requirement to personal option that deals life or death, every second of our lives, depending on our own conscious choices.

3

Celibacy as a Sign of Human Possibility

Celibacy challenges assumptions about the values of the world and the society in which we live. It deflates conventional wisdom. Examining this challenge, we can understand how celibacy operates as witness to a gospel that seeks to draw our consciousness from that which is present into that which is not yet accomplished.

Celibacy proclaims our belief in what is not yet evident to the eye of the intellect: a future possibility hidden within the depths of the person. The actualization of this possibility was made manifest in the mystery of the life, death, and Resurrection of Jesus Christ, who, through that mystery, fully realized the human capacity to love unconditionally. Into that mystery all Christians have been baptized, and all are likewise called to continue bringing the mystery to fullness. Celibacy is one way some Christians have chosen to express this universal vocation.

Because celibacy contradicts and repudiates conventional wisdom, persons choosing the celibate life are making a challenging statement to the society in which they live. From the genital-sexual point of view, celibates surrender the propagation of their lives and the continuance of their personal identity to oblivion. They cut themselves off from any continuity of life that extends into future generations, staking everything on the span of life that is theirs alone. There will literally be no future generation to carry on their dreams, to finish what they have begun. For them, everything is now.

To get a glimpse of what celibacy is all about, we need only look within the context of the myth of salvation history personified in Abraham and Sarah, who initiated a new current of history and began a journey towards a new destiny, one that could not be imagined or predicted within the norms of their contemporary wisdom (Gen. 12.1-3). At best, that new destiny was only vaguely perceived or, at times, not perceived at all, even by Abraham and Sarah or by those with whom they shared their mysterious journey into the future. They had only the promise, and that promise became their anchor. It is there that we begin to see celibacy within the context of the Judeo-Christian ascesis. In a very real sense, celibate persons today continue to respond to a voice that calls them to leave the natural progression of history, to step aside from the dictates of contemporary folk wisdom, and to enter a way not understood or even imagined as being possible by contemporary society.

Celibate living is a symbol that contains the essence of the meaning of Christianity and its fulfillment in time. Christianity itself, in a broader but no less radical sense, challenges and repudiates the assumptions of conventional wisdom based on what is obvious and immediate, on what we can see or grasp with the senses and with the physical part of our being. Popular wisdom assumes that if we have more, we are more; the more we have and the more we are, the more we live and exert power over the environment, over the fates and destinies of friends, over our enemies, over creation itself. It is directly in the center of those assumptions that the challenge of Christian celibacy is focused.

Even though we speak of celibacy as both a sign and an idea, it is much more than either word suggests. More than an idea, it is a reality that occurs within a person existing at a given time and place; it needs a subject to give it life. It is more than a sign existing apart from the reality to which it points; the sign of celibacy exists within the stream of conscious human history by grasping at an individual human existence. It is the celibate person who, first and foremost, is confronted by the challenge of celibacy. Celibacy repudiates, as folly, the false assumptions of the world as they exist within persons. And it cuts to the core of human relationships as it calls celibates to be the reality of the sign professed.

Throughout the Hebrew and Christian covenants, the revelation of the Creator is altogether affirmative of humanity and creation in general. All of creation is regarded as God's handiwork, a reflection of God's inner, creative life (Gen. 1.18,21,25; Ps. 139). Creation is a song, a word of praise to the Creator. In the unfolding of creation we encounter the ongoing self-revelation of the Creator. The first command given to humanity by God is to care for creation and to be generative of new life. Sexuality is the gateway through which human life continues on its evolutionary path. Human sexual activity is perceived as a means of intimacy and cooperation with the creative life of God. Men and women show forth Godlike qualities in their role as co-creators, giving and nurturing human life. To be sexual, to be physical is, in a sense, to be godlike; it is to share in the life-giving qualities of God. Sexual activity, within the context of God's law, is a prayer of praise and adoration, a sign of God's presence in generative action through human cooperation. Sin is never attributed to sexuality or sexual activity in itself, but only to a misappropriation of that sacred activity for selfish purposes.

With the Incarnation of the Word of God, celibacy and virginity entered the conscious stream of the Judeo-Christian tradition. Previously, sexual activity had been a way of achieving humanity's godlike potential; now abstinence from sexual generativity was seen as an alternative means to the same end. Jesus Christ brought a dramatically altered perception to the notion of a salvific relationship with God, the Creator. And he added a new dimension to the perception of the extent of human life and human sexuality.

Here we must address the issue of the superiority of virginity or celibacy over matrimony and legitimate sexual intercourse. The words *superior* and *inferior* are value terms. When we use them in relation to celibacy and marriage, we are betraying a deepseated and longstanding suspicion of pleasures of the body and of material creation in general. In fact, those terms often disguise an outright rejection—or, at least, a suspicion—of creation, particularly of the body and its sexual nature. The end result of this unfortunate misunderstanding is that we live with a subtle denial of the dignity of marriage and procreation. Such denial erodes our understanding of celibate sexuality and sabotages the development of healthy, life-giving celibate witness in the Church.

The problem might be addressed quite simply by stating at the outset that the terms *superior* and *inferior* do not address the issue at all. Terminology has been a source of difficulty all along, because attempting to put celibacy and marriage in opposition to one another overlooks the real issue and misses altogether the meaning of each state of life in itself and in relation to the other. The terminology reflects a serious error in the understanding of biblical anthropology, which merged into Christian thinking several centuries after the apostolic era and only after it had spread into pagan cultures and had absorbed non-Biblical, non-Christian philosophies. While Christ himself remained celibate, he did not advocate the same for his immediate followers, who, as we pointed out earlier, remained married. Celibacy as a way of life came into prominence only during the fourth century and then as a freely chosen way of expressing one's desire to follow Christ and serve him in the community with more freedom. It was seen simply as another way—not a better way, except for the person choosing it. Only later did some writings begin to describe celibacy as superior to marriage. Those writings were not so much an example of theological development as a departure from Biblical teachings, brought about by non-Christian influences.

It may be helpful to remind ourselves that celibacy neither repudiates nor invalidates the very real value of genital sexual activity in the Christian context; rather, it attempts to draw human love to a more complete dimension of itself. That dimension is already contained in sexual activity when it becomes the ecstatic experience of being drawn beyond the boundaries of one's isolated self into a loving unity with another.

Human consciousness grows, enlarges, and deepens as humanity moves through its history. As a result, humanity becomes aware of realities that were always present but not recognized because of the particular condition and level of development at a given time in our historical process. The idea of celibacy as a viable option for humanity can be considered as merely an extension of thought along a continuum of possible realities, all of which are related and connected to one another as parts to a whole. Progress in human consciousness is always rooted in the past, summarizing it, refining it, and bringing it to a new level of development. Celibacy contains and sums up human genital sexuality and the chaste love it leads to, just as human genital sexuality contains and points towards the development of the possibility of chaste celibacy which does not diminish the capacity to live in true, life-enhancing relationships. Celibacy, no less than matrimony, is a way of being sexual and generative of life. It is a way of encountering God within a community of sexual persons and engaging in a relationship with God, who calls us to give life just as he has given us life.

God is not contradictory. What is good and a blessing one day does not become a curse the next. The blessing simply grows and enlarges so as to reach broader horizons and more profound depths. Therefore, in attempting to understand the spirituality of celibacy, it is essential to keep in mind that celibacy finds meaning and relevance insofar as it addresses itself to the revelation of God through Jesus Christ, a revelation that is directed to all of humanity, enlarging our understanding of what it means to be fully human. In no way can this revelation repudiate or nullify that which preceded it and brought it to the present level. Nor can it call into question or cast suspicion on the dignity and goodness of any aspect of our humanity, through which we are called to serve God in human relationships.

Celibacy makes sense and is right only insofar as it finds its roots in the Gospel message, incarnating that message in such a way as to make it relevant and dynamic to a human society that is searching for light and understanding about itself and its place in the larger scheme of things. If celibacy is truly rooted in the Gospel, it draws out the message of the Gospel, enabling it to reach into the day-to-day reality of human life. The Gospel cannot deny or reject any dimension of our humanity. It cannot call into question or lay suspicion over creation, for creation is a source of divine revelation, as is the totality of the human person. On the other hand, it can and does seek to reject that which diminishes our humanity. It seeks to free us from the bondage that suffocates our true potential and inhibits growth towards the fullness of the godlike qualities inherent in our humanity.

The Incarnate Word of God was sent to awaken the human consciousness and call it to actualize its potential to live in the fullness of love. The Word opens the eyes of our spirit to see and believe in the reality and possibility of that which is beyond our here-and-now vision and understanding. Our humanity is charged and energized by the God-life within us, moving us toward that reality (Gen. 1:1- 2:25). St. Paul prayed that the fullness of God's own life live in us (Eph. 3:19). Likewise, St. John equated love with the very being of God and reminded us that to know love is to know God. To be deprived of love is to be deprived of the experiential knowledge of God (1 Jn. 4). Genuine love makes us truly human, and, in our humanity, God is present and active. Chaste sexual engagement does not contain, restrict, or define the dimensions of human love; rather, sexual engagement releases love for an abiding, humanizing experience that transcends time and place and extends into eternity. Likewise, celibacy that is true and chaste does not inhibit or diminish one's capacity to love and relate to others, but it directs that capacity beyond an exclusive proprietary relationship to a covenanted one with God through life-giving relationships with creation.

The potential that lies beyond the horizon of our minds includes the history of our human journey until the present. We have existed from all eternity in the heart of God—not merely as a created species, but by name, as individuals. The creator has known each of us, has drawn us to life, sustained us, and guided us to this very moment (Ps. 139). When we are born, we are thrust into the history of all humanity; we gather that up in our lives and continue it on its way as we move into and take up the process of our own history. Human history waits to be brought to a new possibility in the life of each of us. At every moment there is new potential waiting to be brought into actuality, even though it might lie beyond our limited perception. The present moment grows and reaches towards its fullness in the future, at times through incredible absurdity, even through evil and the abysmal failure of the Cross.

The Eternal Word of God comes to break us out of the isolation of the moment, to free us from the bondage of the solitary event, and to call us to an awareness of the transcendent reality of our lives. The Word enlarges our awareness of the fact that each moment is dynamic, growing, and reaching for completion. Each event, each moment is rooted in the eternal, creative possibility of God. Ultimately, each moment will break through into the fullness of life and meaning in its unity with the Creator. In all reality, the Kingdom is now, in our midst, coming to completion in our history.

Christ came as one like us, living in humanity, yet in the true union with the Creator that all human beings are created and destined for (Col. 1:15-20). He lived in the intimacy of hope and trust that opened his mind and heart to the "beyond" of the present moment, to the "greater than" of any event or experience. That intimacy is not intended to be suggestive of the split-level mind that some theologians have invented and attributed to Christ in order to protect the integrity of his divine nature and, therefore, his omniscience with the Creator. It is, rather, the same vision of hope and faith that was so very active in Abraham, Sarah, Moses, the Prophets, and Mary. That vision was brought to completion, to its fullest perfection, in Christ on the Cross. It is offered to us as a real possibility for our lives and actions (Eph. 3.16- 19).

Through his death in total, pure love, Christ completed the human journey into the fullness of God's own divine life. In his divine-human nature, Christ is the truth of our humanity. He is "the Way, the Truth and the

Life" for each of us walking in darkness into the fullness of life in love (Jn. 14.6). His sense of self and his relatedness to God through right human relationships were the normal fruits of a life of prayer and faith. His total awareness of reality was the same as that which flooded the consciousness of the martyrs, enabling them to lay down their lives in the sure hope that they were, thereby, entering into the fullness of life in, with, and through the life, death, and Resurrection of Christ.

Christ lived in time and history, passing through events and experiences just as we do. In his vision and awareness, history, experience, and event were drawn into the fullness of all time and eternity in the Creator. So was Abraham's faith brought to its fullness in Christ, who entered into the darkness so that he might lead us to the light.

Celibacy emerges from the mystery of Christ and his relationship with God as a statement of self- understanding. It is a word that articulates what lies beyond and beneath the limits of reason, out of reach of logical, verbal formulas. Celibacy comes forth and stands as a sign that there is something beyond, something more, something not yet identifiable but no less real. Even now, it is in the process of coming to be, and its being is firmly rooted in the earthiness of sexual humanity. When it is finished, it will contain the full realization of our sexual humanity in its completed, perfect form.

The life, death, and Resurrection of Christ contain everything to which his celibacy pointed. In his Resurrection, everything that went before is accomplished and brought to an eternal unity with and in the life of God. The expeience of completion in the unity of God is not discontinuous with the experiences of past time, but it gathers them up, enlarges, and reveals the fullness of meaning in them.

To experience the Resurrection of Christ as the disciples and Apostles did is to glimpse the reality of the beyond, of that which lies on the far side of death and past the limits of what anyone can see and know in the present.

The celibacy of Christ was the sign that pointed humanity in the direction of post-Resurrection reality. In the Resurrection, Christ entered into the reality in which men and women will no longer be given in matrimony, but will live beyond, in the completion of their human sexual partnership. Death and Resurrection are the realization of that ecstatic moment of oneness with another human being extended beyond physical limits to the ultimate source and end, without in any way breaking the connection with the events, persons, and experiences that marked its journey to fulfillment. In that sense, celibacy attempts to point from within the flesh of our humanity to that which lies beyond the present reality, even the present possibility of our humanity, to the fulfillment of all that is human, the divinization of all humanity in full unity with God.

Human genital sexuality is a sacrament that contains and makes present the reality of the intimate participation and cooperation of God and humanity in the ongoing work of creation. To place celibacy in opposition to human sexuality is, in effect, to violate that sacrament of unity. The ultimate effect is to remove the celibate presence from the area of human affairs and to make of it an irrelevancy and a contradiction.

Only in the reality of the Resurrection did all of the pieces fall into place and the questions surrounding the life of Christ suddenly become a statement. The Resurrection event and his post-Resurrection appearances made present in the lives of the disciples, in a very tangible way, the full reality and dimension of the human experience of Christ and, therefore, the full and complete experience of all humanity, namely, the extension of human life beyond the curtain of death into the fullness of the life of God. As a result of the Resurrection event, as well as the post-Resurrection appearances, human consciousness made a quantum leap to a fuller awareness of the extent of human life. The grave no longer marked the end of a life span; it became only the beginning of full life in union with the Creator of all life. Thereafter, the begetting of heirs to carry on one's name and fortune, one's life, one's identity, and one's being into future generations took on a new context. Awareness of what it meant to be procreative and, through procreative action, immortal was pushed past the old barriers, so that existence now encompasses more than birth, puberty, marriage, procreation, and death. Each life now is seen in the context of the eternal.

This change has ramifications for sexual procreation. The begetting of life now has an eternal dimension. Procreative activity is seen as a sacrament whereby man and woman participate in a cooperative encounter with a god who creates life in his image, life that has an eternal dimension, life that—even in flesh and time—is rooted in the eternal now. Thus, personal immortality is not dependent on heirs and human accomplishments, but is inherent and complete in individual lives, each of which contains and describes the mystery of eternity in time, of immortality in human flesh, and of the divinizing process going on and being realized, even now, as we interact and seek to bring meaning and unity to our human existence.

In effect, the celibacy of Jesus calls Christians to take their sexuality seriously because it is a sacrament of eternal life in the Creator. Christ-centered celibacy announces and points to the eternal and transcendent dimension of human activity, to that transcendence which is hidden but functioning and dynamic, even now in our most earthy human actions. If Christian marriage makes present in sacramental form the real, creative, life-giving presence of God in human life and covenanted sexuality, covenanted celibacy makes present and announces the Kingdom where eternal love begins in human flesh. Within our enfleshed humanity it grows and matures into free, nonpossessive relationships, continuing beyond bodily expressions and bodily forms into participation in God's eternal love.

In order to understand a Christian spirituality of celibacy, we need to consider the model, Jesus Christ, and to remember that our celibacy is rooted in his understanding of himself and his relationship with God. It was his relationship with God that oriented his entire relatedness to humanity and creation. In a word, his entire life spoke and pointed to the truth of all humanity, of every person without exception. His life—and his celibacy was a pronounced characteristic of his life—spoke to humanity of the breadth, depth, and height of human potential that was, even then, being realized in him and being called into full actuality in all of humanity (Col. 3:1-4).

Jesus' celibacy was a way of engaging in the human predicament. It was a sign that pointed from the human predicament to the fullness of human love. It still calls us to be aware that human love and sexuality are on a progressive continuum, moving into life in the Kingdom—even now and from here, where we struggle with a condition that is not yet fully redeemed or complete.

Jesus' celibate relationship to people brought a new dimension into their lives and called attention to the deeper reality of human love that included, but was not contained by, the physical and temporal in the center of their being. It brought them to the solitary center that no human love can ever enter or hope to satisfy.

Rooted in Jesus Christ, the celibacy of the Catholic priest, religious, or lay person points to the reality that is constantly being called into actuality within the depths of the person. Externally, the reality of the celibate is surrounded by cultural and legal accouterments. Internally and subjectively, celibacy is qualitatively conditioned by the subjective psycho-sexual reality of the person. However, the individual who is celibate for the Kingdom stands in the community as a sign reminding us that our lives, all of them, are moving past the given moment of incompleteness or the brokenness of sin to fulfillment of a promise that is rooted in our brokenness and is being mysteriously realized in the actual condition in which we find ourselves.

In the rich imagery of the Book of Revelation, Ch. 5, the earthly experiences of the suffering and death of Christ constitute the heavenly glory of the Lamb. Christ embraced and suffered the weak, limited, broken condition of humanity in order to show us that the promise of salvation begins within the reality of humanity and, through that reality, draws us to full union with God. In Christ, celibacy was a sign that pointed to the reality in him; in ourselves, celibacy is a sign of hope in the promise that is, even now, coming to fullness from within our subjective experience of celibate sexuality.

If celibacy is a sign of the coming fullness of the Kingdom in our lives, the Kingdom that is being established within us even as we experience our sinfulness, it must necessarily bear the imprint of our human condition. It is a bold sign, because while it is, in one sense, tarnished by our own sinfulness, it continues to hold out the promise of what can be and will be. Our sinful, incomplete condition is the seedbed out of which we grow into unity with Divine Love.

Healthy celibates, then, do not fear or disdain human weakness; neither do they attempt to stand aside, distant and remote, as though untainted by the earthy side of their humanity; rather, because they are in touch with and accepting of the reality of human frailty and inadequacy, they are engaged in a genuine relationship of compassion for others. Mature celibates are grounded in trust in the basic goodness of all creation, not excluding humanity because of its sexual nature. It is precisely because of their experience of the promise being realized in their own sinfulness that they are able to be dynamic, tangible agents of that promise to others who are struggling with the inadequacies and limits of their married or single state.

Together, in a community of persons who are aware of their present limitations and the poverty of their efforts, the Christian married person and the Christian celibate support and enable one another to live in the promise, knowing that the promised Kingdom is not separate or alienated from their present condition and experience, but rooted in and being actualized, even now, beyond their knowledge and perceived experience. Christ did not enter the lives of human beings to make them feel ashamed, guilty, or anxious about their present condition and their experiences of sinfulness. Much less was his unmarried state an occasion for them to feel inferior. Rather, he made them aware of their potential for holiness by his total and unqualified acceptance of them as brothers and sisters. In forgiving, being forgiven, and loving one another, they too could hope to realize the truth of their person in renewed relationships. In short, he freed them from undue fear and anxiety over their sin and brought peace in the freedom of knowing that they were loved and called to live in love with one another.

4

The Spirituality
of Celibacy

Too often in the past and frequently enough in the present, we come across a notion of spirituality that attempts to disassociate our relationship with God and the things of God from the nitty-gritty of our daily lives. We see reluctance to allow God to reveal himself and to engage in the day-to-day encounter with our earthiness. But such reluctance is inconsistent with divine revelation as it speaks of God's faithfulness to us throughout our history of sin and infidelity. Within that reality God meets us and calls us to be open to divine intervention, so that he can be a creative presence with us, bringing completion and fullness to our experience of life.

In Genesis, we find an image describing the inspired author's understanding of what it means to be a human person. When God breathed his own life into the stuff of creation, humanity came to life in union with the life of God, to become the sacrament of God's living presence in creation (Gen. 1.26-27, 2.7). The essence of our human nature is to be in relationship with God and creation; we are the point of encounter between Creator and created. Thus, we were made the stewards of earth and the things of earth, including the human family. In right relationship with God and creation, we are the co-creators whereby the divine plan for the fulfillment of creation is accomplished.

It is our life within a body-mind-spirit unity that makes us consciously present to and in relationship with the world around us. It is our spirit that enables us to go beyond the physical boundaries of our bodies so as to make contact and interact with the "not I." Spirituality is primarily relational. Our place in the scheme of things is discovered and worked out from within the context of relationships. We cannot even be aware of or know ourselves except in relation to persons, places, things, times, and events. We exist in conscious relationship to the rest of creation, all aspects and dimensions of it. Spirituality is not primarily a religious pose that is characterized by a creedal position or circumscribed by and contained within dogmatic beliefs, rituals, or devotional practices. Rather, it is rooted in the essence of humanity and prior to a religious structure. Any religious structure, whatever its ritual times, places, and devotional practices, must proceed from that reality and be directed towards enabling right and true relationships, beginning with oneself, extending to others, to creation, and to God.

Spirituality is a way leading to a point in divine life where our minds and hearts are opened to an awareness that all things are one in God; that separation, "otherness," the "not I" are, in fact, delusions. Therefore, when we speak of Christian spirituality, we need to address ourselves to the quality of our relationships to self, as well as to other persons, places, things, events, and circumstances. There is no single dimension of our relationships that is insignificant or irrelevant. Every relationship speaks to us of the quality of our spirituality and, ultimately, of the quality of our relationship with God, as well as the quality of our life in general. Divine revelation is God's initiative in guiding us towards right relationships. To ignore that dimension of the Christian message is to completely misunderstand and, therefore, to distort the meaning of Christianity at its heart.

A spirituality of celibacy finds its life in the opening of our relationships to the light of divine revelation. Celibacy is a way of life-giving relationships with men and women and, ultimately, with all of creation. Any less positive view allows easy entry to unhealthy, negative, self-serving pseudospirituality, which, in turn, tends to reinforce poor psychosexual development and to remove the possibility of further growth and development that is necessary for true, life-giving celibacy.

It was observed earlier that the celibacy of Jesus is a characteristic sign pointing to a total inner reality. The reality pointed to is the mystery of Jesus' life in and with God. That relationship was incarnate and imminent but, at the same time, transcendent and eternal. It was rooted in his human nature, yet it extended beyond, to the very heart of the Creator. It began in time and continued into eternity. Because Jesus' celibacy was an incarnate reality—rooted in his humanity, but pointing beyond his present condition to the fulfillment of all that his humanity was—his human condition stands as a reminder of the fulfillment that is coming to be right now.

Jesus is the true, fully realized mystic whose vision and awareness not only embrace the present moment, the present limited, human conditon, but also go into the depth, width, and breadth of this moment to see and embrace what is coming to be. He sees and embraces the whole truth of the present moment and the present condition. Most important to realize, however, is that people of his time experienced him as being totally with them, not disengaged and distant. It was obvious from their reaction to his presence that they did not experience themselves as being condemned or criticized, but as being totally welcomed into a relationship that energized and affirmed them. That welcome and affirmation did not exclude the broken, sinful side of their lives, but brought it into a healing relationship of forgiveness and reconciliation. Jesus' celibate relationship to himself, to God, and to other people was integral and complete; It drew others into the same unity, enabling them to experience the promise of their own lives. It opened them to a life of hope.

Jesus Christ is like us in all things but sin—in all things: in our limitations, in our vulnerability, at times even in our darkness and absurdity; but not in our sin, because he did not allow the darkness and limitations of our hidebound perceptions to entrap him in the perceived limitations of the historical moment and, thus, in hopelessness. His relationships with other people were not self-interested, but self-giving. He brought life and affirmation to his human encounters. He was the promised Redeemer, and in him the promise can be grasped in concrete human terms. All of us can relate to failure and to sin, as well as to the pain of trying to live through failure in hope and in trust. We all know the feeling of being exploited and manipulated through our weaknesses. Likewise, we know the healing and redemptive value of nonjudgmental acceptance and affirmation, as opposed to the guilt and shame that come from judgmental condemnation and blame. Thus, the figure of Jesus dying on the cross, not allowing his human heart to be caught up in the whirlwind of human evil surrounding him, is a consistently powerful image of Christianity. Suffering, death, and resurrection are powerful images in human mythology because we know that they speak intimately to our own experiences of suffering and death.

In the suffering, death, and Resurrection of Christ, we are led past the predicament of the sin and darkness of the moment to the meaning of that moment: the fulfillment of his promise. However, Jesus' experience of the moment does not stop there; it goes beyond, to fulfillment of its inherent promise of life in God. Christ was—and still is, in our bodies—the pilgrim making his way through an uncharted course, becoming the light of that course for us. He makes our experience his own and, from within it, traces the way to the truth of God's mind and heart, of which he is the perfect image; thereby, he becomes for us the Truth. He enters into our lives and, from there, moves into the fullness of life in God. As a result, he became for us the Life; he is "the Way, the Truth, and the Life" (Jn. 14.6). In the Resurrection, he returns to each of us in a mystical relationship, calling us to live in him and to allow him to live and take on flesh again in us (Eph. 1.22-23). His passion, death, and Resurrection must be repeated in our lives, through our faithful surrender in trust to that same vision, so that his body, the Mystical Body of Christ, can continue to come to fullness in time and in history.

His invitation is given to all. To married persons, it means moving towards the fullness of life in God in ways that are consistent with convenanted married love. To persons who are committed to celibacy, the invitation calls for a response that complements the response of those who are married. The common bond that unites both married couples and celibates is that all are called into positive, true, human relationships. Through both responses, the mystery of Jesus' love, his relationship to God, and his mission to the world are present and active. There is no opposition, only complementarity, unity, and wholeness. It is the wholeness of God's unity with the Son, and both in the Holy Spirit, that same Holy Spirit now dwelling in His body, the Church.

It was observed previously that the reality and meaning of celibacy are addressed first to the persons espousing it. In the condition and quality of their lives, they are the first to be confronted and challenged by celibacy as a sign pointing beyond the limits of humanity into full life in God, to the Kingdom that is coming to be. What was realized and actualized in Jesus through his life, death and Resurrection is somehow to occur in the Christian, married or celibate. Marriage, in the Christian sacramental context, incarnates trust in the enduring goodness of creation and the place of human life in that creation, guiding the historical process away from the tyranny of sin to its fullness in the Creator. It does so by faithful adherence to the demands of Christ-centered human love that dies to selfishness, and by the sharing of that love in generation of new life. Christ-centered married love is the seedbed for the virtue of hope in the fulfillment of God's promise, realized in the life of each person. Christ-centered celibacy stands in the midst of the married community in a complementary partnership. It seeks to be a sign of the continuation and completion of the love to which all, without regard to state of life, are ultimately called and for which all hearts long. In the final analysis, all are called to live as parents, generating new life for the Kingdom which begins now and extends into the life of God.

The question for all who are celibate is this: How do we actualize the sign element of celibacy in our lives so that our celibate presence in the community is relevant and effective in extending community consciousness to the full meaning of Christian love? In other words, how do we realize celibacy in our lives so that it continues to make present the sign of Jesus Christ living in persons in right relationships?

Primarily, celibates must be aware of their need to own and incorporate their celibate state into their conscious lives. If they attempt to close celibacy off into a dark corner of consciousness, accepting it only in a superficial and cursory way, they are going to relate to it and experience it simply as the result of circumstances outside of their conscious control, thus not truly relevant to the meaning of their lives or the lives of others around them.

A peculiar set of stress-producing conflicts arises in the ministry and the human relationships of individuals who have accepted celibacy only on a surface level. They never really enter into or understand the mystery of their celibate sexuality and human psychosexual development in relation to spiritual growth and development. They do not realize the effects those conflicts have on their self-understanding and the way in which they interact with the world around them. Yet they do not identify themselves or feel comfortable as celibate persons in a world that values and rewards indiscriminate sexual activity and the narcissistic pursuit of gratification. There remains a space between their condition as celibates and their self-understanding in relation to human society and the world.

Human relationships, even at their best, can become and often do become stress-producing because of the conflicting feelings and tensions they produce. Relationships that develop beneath the surface of cultural conventions eventually rub against the boundaries of defense mechanism and egotistical concerns; therefore, they often accentuate feelings of loneliness, solitude, and alienation. In the proper circumstances, those very feelings can provide the energy for growth towards maturity and responsible human interactions and deep relationships. But a celibate person who is not free to engage in the give-and-take of those struggles—either because of inner psychological inhibitions or through cultural conditioning, perhaps reinforced by distorted religious beliefs—may move into compensatory activities or relationships in an attempt to assuage stressful feelings or avoid meaningful human relationships altogether. Thus, a setting is provided for superficial sexual liaisons that serve only to add a a layer of guilt and a sense of unworthiness or helplessness to an already stressful state.

For persons who, for whatever reason, avoid explicit sexual liaisons, there are other, less dramatic, less socially offensive, but no less harmful kinds of compensatory reactions. Material possessions and comforts can become substitute sex objects or personal immortality symbols that beguile the person into thinking of such things as harmless means of satisfaction in an otherwise empty and unfulfilled life. A freewheeling life-style that becomes an endless round of activities, projects, and enterprises—even religious ones—can lead to a life that is characterized by gross selfishness and narrow-minded preoccupation with personal needs and wants under the guise of ministry and service to others. In extreme cases, such a mode of living can become a cause of scandal and disenchantment as bad as, or worse than, explicit sexual scandal or other forms of disedifying behaviour.

Such negative options and their nonproductive results serve only to highlight the challenge of the celibate commitment to the people of God. The radical nature of that challenge is made manifest in the appearance of the negative and nonproductive options that stand in marked contrast to the positive, life-giving options to which the celibate is called. The condition of celibacy, truly embraced and allowed to develop, calls one to a peculiar set of relationships that are radically opposed to the norms of society and the world. Celibacy highlights both the negative and the positive options that are available to all Christians. It dramatizes the polarity between sin and grace.

Jesus is the Word of God through whom all creation was spoken into existence. He is the absolute truth of creation, the absolute truth of every human person, the truth that is fully actualized in human form, the new Adam, the new creation, made real and present in history. "He is the image of the unseen God and the first born of all creation, for in him were created all things in heaven and on earth: everything visible and everything invisible, Thrones, Dominations, Sovereignties, Powers—all things were created through him and for him" (Col. 1. 15-16). In his human life he was presented with the same options that present themselves to us daily: life or death, light or darkness, sin or grace. Through such choices we determine the quality of our lives and relationships; we either put on the mind and heart of Christ and allow his life to continue through ours or we live in the darkness of our own culturally conditioned egos.

Sin is a reality in creation. But sin does not arise only as a result of our volitional acts and omissions. It is a power that permeates to the center of creation, through the center of human consciousness into the unconscious, the source of creative possibilities that are waiting to be drawn into light and participation in life. It is a power that impedes the progress of creation towards its rightful end, namely, right relationships. The power of sin presents humanity with a system of false values that are rooted in darkness and opposed to the truth of creation as it exists in the mind and heart of the Creator; thus the human person develops a sense of identity, a persona, in an environment that seduces us away from our proper role of revealing and expressing the Image of God. Our sense of self is inflated by the false values of our culture: power, the esteem of others, control, the delusion of individualistic autonomy, and personal immortality.

The temptations of Jesus in the wilderness (Matt. 4. 1-11) present us with an image of the dismantling of the tyranny of sin over our personal ego. In those temptations, Jesus confronted the three major conventional assumptions and value systems that tarnish all human relationships through erosion of human interactions with creation and with other persons. The first temptation, pursuit of bread and all that it symbolizes as the primary value in life, placed personal, individualistic survival and physical well-being above the common good. God's Word challenged that value and placed agape, mutually supportive and caring relationships, before personal survival. The second temptation, which is the most insidious of all deceptions, that of religious corporate power co-opting one's real or imagined relationship with God in order to sustain the inflated personal or corporate ego, was exposed for the lie that it is. We are slow to realize that much of our religious practice and belief, individual as well as collective, is no more than a covering over of our primitive greed and egocentrism. In the third temptation, Jesus' response deflated the commonly held assumption that we can bring about right through political might. In fact, it is another deception of our culturally inflated ego that causes us to believe we can re-create human society according to our own unredeemed image. Through those temptations, Jesus deflated and exposed the lie of the inflated ego grounded in the unredeemed values of the world. By making choices that repudiate worldly conventions, he charted a new course for the development of human consciousness. It was from his encounter with the forces of darkness that he went forth and ascended the mountain to articulate a new paradigm for human relationships, the Sermon on the Mount (Matt. 5-7).

Just as the Ten Commandments reveal not only God's will for human behaviour but also what the human heart is capable of achieving, so too the Sermon on the Mount is a revelation of the truth of the potential of the human spirit. It is an invitation to enflesh the holiness of God in human relationships. By it we are challenged to follow Jesus into the wilderness, to identify and be resposible for the tyranny of sin in our lives, and to come away from that experience to begin the process of living in right relationships.

Christianity, at its heart, is a bold and radical repudiation of the values of a human society that is entangled in the darkness of sin. To follow Jesus, the new Adam, on a course founded on the belief that human beings are inherently capable of transcending greed, violence, and fear; to live in poverty of spirit, non-violence, and freedom—that requires deliberate and conscious choices. Christians, having been baptized into the life, passion, death, and Resurrection of Christ, need to understand that to live out the baptismal commitment is to make personal choices that daily move us more deeply into a personal relationship with God, the Creator, and therefore into a more authentic relationship with the truth of ourselves. That is the beginning of a return to right relationships with society, with the world, and with creation.

Celibate persons must own the decision to live in the celibacy of Jesus Christ, a celibacy that grasps at the core of existence and seeks to transform it into a sign pointing to the reality of a time and a condition in which all human love is drawn into a timeless unity with its source and end. That time does not mark the termination of human love; instead, it marks the fulfillment of love in charity, the charity that begins now in the imperfection and poverty of our lives with one another.

The Christian celibate stands in the midst of the human predicament, experiencing the exquisite loneliness, the poverty, and the limitations— even the sinfulness—of human relationships. From within that predicament the celibate seeks to keep alive the hope of the promise by freely surrendering his or her life in order to become a conscious, living sign of God's power, still operative and present in our history.

It is from within the lived experience of the celibate person that conscious choices are made. The experience of the poverty of sinfulness, loneliness, solitude, and frustration, along with the sense of being an unwelcome, misunderstood, and sometimes suspect presence in a society that understands only self indulgence and power—that is the experience out of which the celibate freely chooses to enter into the mystery of Christ. Therefore, celibates are in the uncomfortable position of having to choose between buying into a value system that they are called to challenge, or standing against it and paying the price of living on the fringe of their culture, of being strangers in their own land.

Celibacy points beyond the limited range of human experience to the depths of the Kingdom in the heart of God. It was Jesus' rootedness in that vision of the truth of things that enabled him to give up all and embrace the darkness of the moment because he saw through it and past it to the ultimate truth: life in the Creator. To live in Christ is to allow his vision of reality to break open the narrow boundaries of our vision and enlarge it so as to include the transcendent reality of the Kingdom happening in our lives even now. Only that vision empowers us to live in and embrace the reality of the given moment and circumstance. The very reality of celibacy places us on the cutting edge of the Christian revelation.

The celibate person has two options: either to live totally committed to the poverty of spirit which celibacy implies, a symbol containing the reality it signifies, the emerging Kingdom breaking through in the midst of the human predicament in all its light and darkness, or to choose to remain uncommitted. Such failure is, in fact, a choice to live in unredeemed solitude, seeking to fill the void with the seductions and empty symbols of a society that is without hope beyond the fleeting moment. It is the ultimate foolishness, like the foolishness of one who gives up all so that the pearl of great price may be purchased, but then neglects to do what is necessary to secure the land that contains the precious pearl (Matt. 13.44). In the end, such a person is left with nothing but desolation.

Celibacy can become a viable, life-giving sign only when we choose to live entirely rooted in Christ and to embrace the folly of the Cross as we experience it, keeping alive the vision of the fulfillment of hope in the Resurrection. In that way, the very substance of our lived existence, our daily experience, becomes an act of adoration and supreme worship. Then the continuation of the mystery of redemption in Christ becomes more than a theological possibility. The substance of our lives and relationships translates it into living flesh and blood.

5

Celibacy: In and For a Community

Part 1

I have stressed that it is the task of the individual to take responsibility for his or her own life so as to grow and mature in self- knowledge and human relationships. Respect for the unfolding mystery of each unique life does not allow for the abdication of personal responsibility for the quality of one's life and relationships. That being said, however, it is necessary to consider the extraordinary power of structural roles and functions in the development of our sense of self and in the options available to us in the course of life.

Celibacy, like matrimony, is not the sole possession or responsibility of the individual who espouses it; it is part of the heritage and tradition of the Christian religion. For that reason, religious leaders have an obligation to monitor the integrity and authenticity of the various social and cultural expressions of celibacy at a given time. In order for it to be a live, authentic expression of Christian revelation, there is need to encourage healthy and relevant circumstances that provide positive support in living its mystery.

Church community, at its best, enhances individual efforts to live productively in celibacy or in matrimony. However, there can be communal attitudes that diminish the fruitfulness of a chosen way of life as an expression of Gospel values. When such attitudes are fixed in the community consciousness over a period of time, they become embedded in the unconscious also, so that they continue to be accepted without critical reflection. Thus they can become cultural conventions, stereotypes that lock individuals into preassigned cultural roles with correspondingly fixed expectations. At one time those roles, with their corresponding functions, might have been realistic in working out personal identity in the community. However, as history continues to call for new structures to meet new needs, there is often a lag between the appearance of these new structures with their changed values and the letting-go of old stereotypes with the corresponding assumptions that have long identified people in groups within the overall cultural context.

Institutions such as the Catholic church, rigidly sectioned into hierarchical groupings, are very efficient in defining roles and establishing norms of behaviour to regulate relationships and interactions between different groups. Too easily some groups become isolated—at times subtly, but no less effectively—in terms of significant social interactions with other groups. Historically, as well as very recently, such isolation has oftentimes resulted in less than healthy consequences.

So it was that the celibate male clergy became a class unto itself, while women and nonordained men religious were virtually isolated from the laity. Each group had its prestige, with corresponding privileges, but all were in a closed system that allowed little or no interaction unless it was controlled by custom and had a predetermined role and function. Communication "downward" to the laity was usually characterized by a maternal or paternal kind of authority. Communication "upward" was often marked by obsequiousness and an air of subservience, whether by the laity towards their clergy and religious, or by clergy and religious towards their clerical or religious superiors.

For the diocesan priest who did not live in a community of peers, the "clerical club" became almost the sole outlet for tensions and, for many, the only source of companionship as well as spiritual nourishment, through priests' prayer groups and retreats. While those groups served a useful and necessary purpose under the circumstances, the relationships were often superficial and guarded, at best.

While members of religious communities enjoyed the internal support of living with the other members of their community, there too the resulting relationships were often superficial, laboring under the control of law and the suspicion of peers and superiors alike. At the same time, outside relationships were usually restricted solely to business matters. Along with the fear of homosexuality or illicit sexual attachments, there was little or no sensitivity or sympathy towards human needs for intimacy and special friendships, which were seen as divisive and disruptive of community life. As the result, many religious and priests lived entirely without human warmth and affection, even without friendship that had little to do with overt sexual involvement.

Ordinaries and religious superiors assumed that if they provided the handbook of rules and made sure that candidates for priesthood and religious life measured up to what was expected of them in formation, all would work out well. If, in fact, someone subsequently caused embarrassment or encountered difficulty, it was assumed that he or she was not keeping the rules. Problems were often dealt with by reassignment and an admonition to "get it together." But, as often as not, changes in assignment were made without so much as a hint of the real reason, leaving the person involved to wonder whether the change was just routine, or if he/she had been "caught."

Human failure was frequently seen as a punishable betrayal of Mother Church and a scandal to the "innocent" laity, rather than as a legitimate and understandable encounter with our commonly shared frailty that calls for healing compassion with understanding forgiveness.

While many in the Church today have made external adjustments to the changes since Vatican II, it seems that others are still living out the unconscious fears and inhibitions that remain conditioned in all of us. Such is the result of the lag between our conscious intellectual shifts in understanding and action and corresponding changes in the unconscious conditioning of the past. We simply have not had time to make the deep shifts in consciousness that are being called for in today's Church and ministry. This, I believe, is the cause of much confusion and tension in religious and clerical circles today.

We are living out of an experience of a Church that did not recognize the value of human relationships in the redemptive process. Celibacy and the virtue of chastity were seen as best served by minimizing human intimacy and controlling necessary and unavoidable human relationships by negative precepts rooted in basic fear and suspicion of human nature.

Admittedly, there are risks involved in human relationships, but it seems excessive to address them by attempting to eliminate them altogether. We have an abundance of convincing evidence that the risks of suffocating the human need and drive towards intimacy are, indeed, just as dangerous and, ultimately, just as damaging as the alternative.

Here we can see the depth of the wisdom and insight of St. Thomas Aquinas, namely, that virtue is balance, harmony, a cooperative interaction between feelings and will (Summa, Q. 151, "Of Chastity"). And we need to remind ourselves that balance and prudence cannot be legislated; to acquit ourselves responsibly according to our chosen obligations remains entirely in the realm of personal freedom and choice. Consequently, in the selection and formation of persons considering a life of celibacy, the focus of attention and effort needs to be the identification of mature persons who show signs of being capable of continuing growth. The process of formation and training can then be concentrated on the development of individuals who are capable of making responsible, independent decisions, with an awareness of their future consequences.

Concupiscence is the tyranny of our sensual appetites set loose from the disciplined restraint of common sense and right reason. Each of us is obligated to inform our consciousness of the right way of living and relating through prayerful listening to God's Word, as well as through our mature and free response to that Word. We can then bring reason and will—formed by a conscious commitment to the Word—to bear on our feelings and desires as we seek to act in a mature, unselfish way according to our freely chosen state of life. Doing that requires not only a healthy asceticism based on a positive sense of self-worth and a realistic assessment of our ability to take responsibility for our decisions and actions but, also, on a healthy and positive discipline of that asceticism, aimed at establishing balance and harmony in all aspects of life.

If—somewhere over the course of one's life—a free, personal decision is made to accept and interiorize the celibate option, to truly be the celibate that one's state in life requires, subsequent sexual desires and feelings will be occasions to more deeply live out that decision. A decision is never a one-time thing; it continues to be actualized and to mature as one lives and encounters options that could conceivably lead to a different course. Each crisis can be regarded as an opportunity to continue living out one's options by making free moral choices that reinforce prior decisions. Fully living out the celibate option is actually a process of altering one's consciousness, altering the quality of one's being and presence in the world. To repeat, that process can never be contained or completed in a simple response to a legal requirement; it must be gradually rooted in the growth of one's psyche and spirit so as to influence the totality of one's life and relationships at the center.

On the other hand, if one is living out the "victim" role, allowing basic decisions to be imposed from "out there" or "up there," then one can quite logically expect difficulty in dealing with the discrepancy that exists between quite normal, legitimate desires and what "they" (God, the Church, superiors, and the community) expect and require. In that state, life is being lived by the decisions and values of others. The gap between the true inner self and the external, social role has never been bridged by a personal moral choice. One's call has never been owned.

A vocation in the real sense happens when one's external life and circumstances reflect inner self-awareness. Thus, a vocation is a lifelong process of personal growth and development, of listening and responding. One's life and actions can be—indeed, must ultimately become—the expression of one's self-awareness. Discontinuity between one's inner sense of self and the external circumstances of one's vocation are the result of failure to take responsibility and claim ownership for life. Celibacy cannot be long sustained on that level. Fidelity to celibacy, just as fidelity in marriage, must be established on a personal and free moral choice that will need to be actualized and lived out every day of one's life. It is here, in this inner space, that prayer and community make the difference, where they become healing, integrating, and life-giving. (cf. PPVI, Encyclical on Priestly Celibacy; Part II, sec. 1, Priestly Formation, par. 72).

In the thinking of St. Thomas Aquinas, to be extreme in the interest of virtue is, in fact, no virtue at all. Thus, to attempt to protect the state of celibacy by eliminating relationships or by separating entire groups of persons from one another is not only counterproductive, but in itself seems to be contrary to the spirit of the virtue of chastity, which seeks to call all of us into a community of right relationships. Therefore, chastity and celibacy have as their ultimate aim the virtue of charity lived in a concrete engagement in and with the world as a community. Any system that has as its purpose the fragmentation of the Body of Christ into exclusive functional units for the purpose of protecting an abstract notion of virtue is missing that point.

Virtue can exist, grow, and mature only in a real person with emotional and social needs. It is the unique, limited, human situation of that person, as well as the unique qualities of the person in normal social relationships, that gives flesh and material presence to virtue. To set up a system that places high value on abstract and academic theories of the ideal of virtue, forgetting the limited, unfinished human person attempting to live out the reality of virtue, is ludicrous. Yet it appears that the Church has fallen into the error of exalting the ideals of chastity and celibacy while paying little attention to the human vessels in which the mystery of those states is being lived out. Abstract and academic ideals of chastity and celibacy have been so romanticized that the queen of all virtues, charity, and the healing fruit of that virtue, compassion, have more often than not been forgotten.

Once we recognize and accept the truth that the Church, its mission, and its vision can become entangled in the capriciousness of human thinking and seduced by fear, then we can set ourselves about the business of calling her to repentance. In the final analysis, the Church, the Body of Christ, the dwelling place of the Holy Spirit, lives and finds her presence in human flesh. In each of us the Spirit waits to be born into new life, new action, through our individual call to be a new creation in Christ. Every time one of us recognizes the tyranny of sin in our lives and relationships, the Church grows and comes to new life in us. It becomes holy in each of us, one person at a time.

Contrariwise, when we consciously or unconsciously relegate the Church to the position of a mere theological abstraction, a bureaucratic entity ensconced in a network of legal and administrative power, then we abdicate personal responsibility for calling the Church to holiness in truth, beginning with the truth of our own lives. If the Church has fallen into sin and been seduced by the demon of authority, power, security, control, unquestioning conformity to cultural conventions—and yes, even religious conventions—that could have happened only because members of the body allowed themselves, albeit unconsciously, to be enticed by the promise of easy salvation.

When one hides within the walls of a political, religious, or socioeconomic class, one's fear of autonomous existence is anesthetized, and one's sense of self becomes invested in that class and its symbols. Christ calls us away from the power of sin that drives us into the isolation of class distinctions. In him we are called to return to right relationships. That is why the central thrust of Christ's message is a call to community, wherein all distinctions of class are done away with. The archetypal image of community is Eucharist, which, when drawn out to its fullest social dimension, extends into intimate, classless social contact and service, as in the washing of the feet (Jn. 13; Col. 3.11).

Our redemption takes place when we truly live the sign of the Eucharist in everyday relationships that look to the real human needs of all of our brothers and sisters. A celibate person, whatever else he or she might be, is first to be a sign of total self-giving and receiving in normal give-and-take within the community. Any kind of class distinction that separates us into isolated, hierarchical compartments is contrary to the full meaning of Eucharistic community. At the same time, the members of the Body of Christ are deprived of the full exercise of their Eucharistic ministry when those from whom they receive ministry are segregated into a privileged class, isolated from the heart of the community. When one segment of the body is divided from the other, the entire body suffers.

The power of sin triumphs when we allow ourselves to be drawn into class relationships, social roles, and functions that inhibit the full flowering of our call to Eucharistic community, as well as the full flowering of our human potential. Humanity is called to the fullness of life in the Eucharistic love of Jesus Christ. To settle for less is sin. Classes—whether religious, political, social, or economic—are simply the mindless, unconscious institutionalization of the sin that divides the human family, the Body of Christ.

The Church is realized and made present in the living flesh of each of her members. The Church is the Body of Christ coming to be, but not yet fully realized because you and I have not yet chosen to totally surrender to this mystery in all of its fullness, not chosen to allow the mystery of Jesus Christ to possess us in every detail and aspect of our lives. As long as even one person remains in the darkness of slavery to sin, the Body of Christ will not be truly realized in its fullness. On the other hand, when individuals decide to live in Christ and allow the divine life to reign, to purify and transform them in their actions and relationships into the mind and heart of Christ, then the Church, as it exists in those persons and as they exist in community, will be drawn to a new level of holiness.

To recognize that, at times, the sinfulness of humanity becomes the dominant value in the policies and decisions of our Church is simply to admit that in the final analysis the Church, the Body of Christ, is incarnate in the life of each of us, from the Pope right down to the most lowly person. To say that church policies, attitudes, relationships, and perceptions are sinful, unjust, and insensitive is but a clear-eyed and honest recognition that we, her Body, have not fully entered into and actualized her holiness in our lives. The ultimate responsibility for the Chruch's growth in holiness rests with you and me in cooperation with the Holy Spirit.

Many of the problems of celibacy faced by the modern Church may be rooted in the unfeeling, spiritless institutionalization of what is, at heart, a gift of the Spirit to individuals seeking a way to express their single-minded pursuit of the Holy.

Any gift of the Holy Spirit is inextricably linked to the uniqueness of the person who receives the gift. It is the role of the Church community to recognize, call forth, and nourish those gifts in the service of the Kingdom. When bureaucratic procedure, Church related or otherwise, seeks to appropriate authority over gifts by assuming that it can make the gift appear by law, violence is going to be done towards persons as well as to the integrity of the gift.

When law and the power of authority take precedence over nurturing in freedom and in trust, we are confronted with the need to reassess our role in correcting the imbalance. The quality of the Church's journey to freedom is dependent on our readiness to take responsibility for the quality of our lives in community.

6

Celibacy: In and For a Community

Part 2

In their longing to escape the hardships and uncertainty of existence in the desert by returning to the security and safety of Egypt, the people of the Exodus experienced unconscious resistance to the responsibility of being a free and self-determined people (Exod. 14.11-12, 16.2-3, 32. 1-35). Freedom is an awesome, sometimes frightening burden on the human spirit, giving rise to a temptation to seek the reassuring protection of a shelter wherein we can be cared for. The Hebrews grew weary of a god who demanded and expected their obedience because he knew them and their potential for holiness and freedom better than they themselves did.

We, too, underestimate our potentiality for holiness and union with the truth of God, projecting an idealized notion of holiness onto people, objects, and institutions. When we accept the promise of our humanity with its potential for holiness, we can discontinue our childish projections onto Mother Church and recognize her as being prone to sin in our sin. We realize that only in the holiness of our lives can her holiness be made real. The holiness of the Church begins and ends with the acceptance of our own vocation to live in total freedom and responsibility for our lives and actions in obedience to God. In that light, I believe that celibacy is a viable and authentic way of giving expression to the freedom of gospel values and of making present in our society the sign of the promise of the Kingdom.

Celibacy is a gift to the Church, the entire body of the faithful. But gifts can be abused by those receiving them; they can be co-opted into the service of limited and self-centered purposes. History is filled with examples of the frequency and ease with which God's call, with its gifts, was turned to capricious uses and narrowed down to the distorted perceptions of humankind. Therefore, we should not be unduly dismayed that the gift of celibacy to the Church is not always perceived and accepted with the dignity and reverence it deserves. I am not speaking of personal infidelities on the part of individual celibates, but of the carelessness of Church authorities and institutions in exercising their stewardship over this gift. We seem to unreflectively take celibacy for granted as some sort of static, always-present reality for which we owe no one any accountability whatsoever. There seems to be an unstated assumption—a judgmental one—that if celibacy "does not work" for someone, the fault, as well as the problem, must lie within that person. The responsibility of authority is then acquitted simply by sending the person away to find whatever help is available. It seems not to occur to anyone that perhaps the problem is a symptom of institutional and communal indifference and fragmented community relationships, as well as of an excessive preoccupation with law and external conventions.

As I have repeatedly stressed, celibacy can be a strong and dramatic sign through which the Body of Christ takes an attitude of contradiction in our hedonistic culture. A gift of the Spirit to the community, it can also be the community's corporate gift to society, through which we make personally present our belief in the transcendent, non-violent dimensions of human relationships. Celibacy, truly lived from the gospel perspective, has the capability of calling to judgment and repudiating the violent, manipulative, possessive, and genitally obsessive values that dominate human relationships in our society. The call to celibacy as a viable and life-giving option for Christians must be offered as a gift to be received, appropriated, and interiorized as one's own. That must be done in the name of and for the good of the entire community, including the secular community, though that secular community might not be disposed to recognize it as viable and relevant to them or to society. We need to rid ourselves of the notion that celibacy is the private prerogative of the individual person or the sole responsibility of institutional legislation. It is neither. Much less is it subject to mere religious convention and piety.

The Church has the power and authority to require celibacy from those who choose to be ordained ministers or to enter conventional forms of religious life. We know she has this power by the very fact that she continues to exercise it and the community—lay, clerical, and religious—accepts it. Admittedly, some people do voice objections or questions about the appropriateness of the requirement. Objections and critical questions notwithstanding, the Church continues to exercise the power with at least the implicit consent of her members. However, the dramatically decreasing numbers of capable young men and women presenting themselves as candidates for ordination or for more traditional forms of religious life may be signalling an end to that implicit consent.

Along with the use of the authority to which the community has given implied consent, the Church has a corresponding obligation that is at least as weighty as the obligations of individuals who espouse celibacy as a way of life. And while she might have the power to require celibacy, it does not follow that she has the gratuitous right, in every case, to unreflectively exercise that power without taking into account universal and prior human values.

The obligations of the leadership of the Church can be understood in three areas of institutional influence: first, recruiting and promoting vocations to religious life and priesthood, which is, in effect, recruiting to the celibate state; second, training and formation; and, finally and probably most importantly, the encouragement of a community environment in which the gift of celibacy can be lived and experienced in a spirit of sharing and mutual support, not in sheltered, exclusive, same-sex enclaves. Within all of those areas we are dealing with social and cultural, as well as subjective psychological realities, not the least of which are the attitudes and perceptions which come unreflectively from our unconscious cultural conditioning.

In the first area of influence it would seem that seminary rectors and staff, vocation directors, ordinaries, and religious superiors have a serious obligation to maintain a benign scepticism and healthy doubt towards those who come forward as candidates for holy orders or religious vows. The decision to remain unmarried and childless for one's lifetime should be accepted only with caution by responsible authorities. For any candidate who is seriously and honestly engaged in working out choices, being challenged should not create serious problems; rather, that should provide a welcome opportunity to probe more deeply and to continue exploring possible options and motivations. Such an interlude of soul-searching should be merely the first of a long series of constructive pauses along the way to a final commitment that, it is hoped, will be made with eyes and heart wide open.

Throughout the process of decision-making, the candidate should be aware that his or her choice is not a purely private matter; ultimately it will affect the entire community, for the gift of celibacy is a community sign, even though it resides in the individual person. Since it is for the community that the gift is accepted, the candidate should expect to be accountable to the community for his or her expression of it. Also, because of the importance of the element of accountability, religious communities and seminaries need to be open to responsible and informed participation by the laity in order to insure that the selection and formation of candidates is not done in a mere ritualistic fashion. Too often already we have seen or experienced the disconcerting dilemma of having self-centered, immature celibate men or women dumped on a hapless parish community.

Basically, ongoing accountability serves two purposes. First, it deconditions the candidate from the idea that he or she is accountable to no one in the matter of celibacy. In particular, it encourages examination of ideas or assumptions that might need to be modified and brought into a broad community dimension in order to offset any misogynous tendencies that may be present in the candidate. In the second place, accountability to a community serves to draw the person's consciousness to a new level of awareness of his or her place in and ministry to that community. Accountability stimulates an awareness that celibacy is a communal concern, lived and shared in a community comprised both of married and celibate people who have a stake in the ongoing mission of the Church. Accountability provides a kind of challenge that will dramatically confront any egocentric or narcissistic tendencies. It should be a part of a larger process of identifying and forthrightly dealing with unhealthy propensities that might possibly lead to tragedy later on (PPVI, Priestly Celibacy, Part II, Sec. 1, par. 64).

Celibacy is a reality that emerges out of a mystery, the deep, imponderable mystery of God commingling with our flesh-and-blood existence, through which we are called to give witness to a radical new set of values that repudiate and call to judgment the values of the world in which we live. Those worldly values and attitudes are embedded in our unconscious from the earliest moments of life. They manifest themselves in more or less subtle ways—through our relationships, decisions, and actions. They must be identified and challenged, first, in our own lives and relationships. But the process is not a cognitive, rational one that can be reduced to intellectual formulas or personal volition. The celibate option must be nourished in mystery, in the deep, silent solitude of inner awareness. The celibate option, which originates in the will and mind, needs to be allowed to sink its roots into the deeper levels of the developing psyche and then to draw us into transformed relationships. This can happen only through reflective, prayerful silence, solitude, and meditation. Through a deepening and expanding awareness of our participation in the divine life in the midst of our own daily living, the divine energies within us will be able to nourish our celibate option into a living witness to the divine mystery.

Seminars, workshops, reading lists, discussion groups do not bring about persons of wisdom, nor do they of themselves bring about the deep, inner conversion called for in the Gospel. Nothing can take the place of a personal encounter with God, living and being revealed through our personal lives and experiences. So it is that the second sphere of influence in which the institutional Church needs to examine its obligations towards the nourishment of celibacy is in the seminary or religious house itself. Until seminaries and houses of formation become places where personal union with God is nourished in silence and solitude, we will not be providing wise and mature ministers who come forth and relate to others from a personal experience of God and are living and creating from that lived experience.

No one can realistically find serious fault with the quality of the academic training in seminary or religious education today. If there is a problem, it appears to be one of focus and emphasis, rather than of quality of effort. This came about during the time when the Tridentine seminary was becoming firmly fixed as the model for all priestly training. As a result of an effort to develop theological study as a valid and true science, the emphasis moved away from the contemplative and mystical dimensions of our faith and belief. The scientific model became a major influence, even in the study of mystical theology and the history of Christian spirituality. Intellectual knowledge of God and the spiritual journey became a substitute for the experience of God.

Pope Paul VI observed, quite forthrightly, that oftentimes the difficulties encountered in the observance of chastity stem from a type of formation which does not always adequately reflect the changes that have occurred over the past several years (PP. VI, Encyclical Letter on Priestly Celibacy, Part II, 1, Priestly Formation, par. 60).

In their training, candidates for a life of celibacy must encounter an environment that recognizes the need for prayer on more than a ritualistic, formal, and legal level. As St. Thomas has warned us, the only justification for a life of celibacy is for that life to become more productive and life-giving than if the celibate had married and begotten children. That must involve more than just work and study. Celibacy is not an end in itself; the simple state of being unmarried and childless does not, in itself, add anything to one's ministry or place in the Church. The celibate must compensate for the fact that his or her life will remain unfruitful on the physical level by living in a way that will bear fruit for the Church and the world on a spiritual level.

If the Church is to continue requiring that priests remain celibate in order to minister in the Church, she must accept the obligation to make sure that persons seeking candidacy for priesthood are psychologically, emotionally, and spiritually equipped to bear the burdens of celibacy in a healthy, positive way. The gift of celibacy must be congruent with the candidate's developing self-awareness if it is to be an aid to his or her self-expression in ministry. But law cannot make this happen. The discovery and nourishment of the gift of celibacy is a delicate and sensitive task of discernment that cannot be routinized. Candidates must be realistically aware of their potential for normal growth and development, with ability to relate to and interact with all persons in the community, not just with one sex, age group, or class within that community. Moreover, formation programs need to provide opportunities for growth and development in deep, personal prayer. That will require opportunities for experience in personal silence and solitude, for learning to live in communion with the inner self so as to minister and relate from that center. Likewise, candidates must show signs of ability to deal constructively and creatively with the stresses associated with silence and solitude. Such ability is essential for any normal human growth and development, no matter what one's chosen state in life; yet we can question whether seminaries, as they are presently constituted, are providing an opportunity for genuinely healthy maturation in this respect. In a memorably prophetic statement made to the American bishops gathered for their annual meeting in Washington,

D.C. in November, 1975, the Most Reverend Jean Jadot, the Apostolic Delegate in the United States, made some points relevant to this issue.

In commenting on the community aspect of our prayer, he stated:

Our approach to prayer cannot be changed by external regulations; it must spring from within our hearts. It must be the sincere and authentic expression of our desire to partake of the living sacrifice, the Paschal Mystery of our Lord and Saviour.

He added, "In addition to our role as leaders of liturgical prayer, we must answer our people who more and more are asking us, as the Apostles asked Christ: *Doce nos orare.*"

The young as well as the old are expecting from us guidance and initiation into private prayer. They want us to show them how to meet the Lord in the privacy of their hearts, how to respond to the promptings of the Holy Spirit.

And, finally, he puts forth a sobering question that is just as relevant today as it was in 1975, perhaps more so. "Are we, bishops and priests, willing and, if willing, are we able to lead our people into the ways of real, deep, continuous communion with Christ?" The Holy Father gives us the answer: "what is often most needed is not so much an abundance of words as speech in harmony with a more evangelical life' (Exhortations on the Fifth Anniversary of II Vatican Council, 1970)."

A call to celibacy is a call to prayer, to union with God. For seminaries to direct so much effort toward intellectual and professional preparation while leaving the most important phase of personal development to chance or, at best, to haphazard attempts is certainly a scandal that reverberates throughout all levels of church life and perpetuates itself in future generations.

The best place to prepare young people for ministry in the heterogenious community is, in fact, in a realistic engagement with and as a part of that community. The present seminary system and, to some extent, the formation programs in communities of men and women are largely established and structured according to an attitude that looks upon the world as evil, a place of danger to the candidate. The implication is that one who seeks to be a priest or religious needs to be protected from the rough-and-tumble of the workaday world. Such an attitude automatically signals to the laity that they have chosen the lesser good by remaining in a world of questionable value. Thus, a subtle but dramatic and harmful division has been established between ministers and those ministered to. Until we come to terms with that negative and erosive attitude towards the things, places, and activities of the world, we are going to be seriously disadvantaged in our attempts to address them in a positive and constructive manner. Celibacy, as modeled for us by Jesus Christ, is neither a repudiation nor a condemnation of human sexuality and life in society; it is a radical statement of affirmation of the total spectrum of human sexuality and human relationships. Until we accept that fact, we are going to have a difficult time establishing our relevance and credibility. As long as young people see examples of celibacy that is lived negatively, without joy, spontaneity, creativity, and enthusiasm for life, they will not be inclined to explore the celibate way as a viable option for themselves. When we love and reverence the world as good, as the place where God's Spirit is at work, bringing about the completion of creation through the evolutionary process, then our contemplative solitude will lead to a more dynamic and creative engagement in our ministry of proclaiming the Good News.

If the Church is going to continue to require celibacy of ordained ministers and if religious congregations desire to maintain their credibility, they must re-examine their priorities and recognize that they are committed, not only to intellectual excellence and professional expertise—both of which are important—but, also and essentially, to making present in the world a very real sign of the Kingdom that is not yet present but is coming to be. There is no room for compromise, no alternative to being joyful, positive, and adventurous as contemplatives and mystics in the world. The reality of the Kingdom must be a true, living experience that permeates and transforms our consciousness and broadens our perceptions to include an optimistic vision of human life and endeavor. The genuine minister of the Church is one who is charged with a positive vision of what is possible for the world and for human society. Any solution less than total giving- over to the mystery of the sign we profess will be disastrous, not only for the individual who attempts to carry it out, but for the Church and society as well.

I have tried to point out that neither the institutional Church nor the individual person has an unquestioned right to celibacy. Thus, the authorities of the Church who are called to act in the name of the community have no right to unreflectively encourage or require individuals to embrace the celibate option without, at the same time, assuring that the environment in which it will be tested and ultimately lived is one that will encourage and nourish the person in healthy, life-giving relationships. We need to re-establish the primacy of the contemplative and mystical dimension of prayer and liturgical worship, together with theological study, as being not inimical to professional and academic excellence and normal living in society, but complementary to it. Contemplative presence to the ongoing mystery of God will draw together and integrate theology with personal, ongoing experience in life and ministry. Such integration can only happen in a representative community of men and women who share their lives with one another, who celebrate the Word of God and proclaim his presence in power and service to the world without class, distinction, or privilege save that of humble service and growth in God's own life and love.

The third and most crucial area of concern is the community to which the priest or religious is sent to serve, to live in and be a part of—a community comprised mostly of married persons who are working and raising families as they seek to make contact with their God and bring their lives into some kind of unity.

Oftentimes the young religious or priest is dropped from the seminary or formation house treadmill into an environment with tasks and expectations, roles and functions that are only remotely—if at all—related to what went on in the years of formation. Formation almost always takes place in an environment that excludes a plurality of values, attitudes, and thoughts. Likewise, the formation group is usually made up of persons of the same sex, same socioeconomic class, more or less the same age and educational background, and with the same religious beliefs. Certainly such a stable, protected environment has its positive aspects in that it provides opportunities to discover and strengthen one's self-identity and to develop a sense of values that is clear and focused. But there are negative aspects, also, that could become the seedbed for future difficulties. We must not allow ourselves to forget that it is possible to lose one's skill for interacting with a heterogeneous community in which are represented different ages; broader, more varied experiences; more varied, and sometimes superior educational backgrounds; different religious values (perhaps more realistic because free from abstract theologies and idealistic star gazing); and, of course, the opposite sex. It is in such a community that the young celibate is expected to spend the rest of his or her life in ministry. That is the real world, the environment where God is intervening in the flow of human history and human relationships, revealing himself in truth, calling us to live, act, and relate in truth, and to continue the divine plan of creation in our lives and actions.

All too often, after years of study in an academic setting, the young celibate becomes spiritually disconnected from the experience of the living God who reveals himself not only in theologies or philosophies, but also in the daily unfolding of the mundane life of raising children, getting to work on time, and getting the shopping done between car pool assignments. Thus, the prayer, study, and reflection of formation needs to be always moving in the direction of placement in and integration with the larger community. Holiness lies in being related, in recognizing our place within the context of the whole, in the giving of our gifts as well as the receiving of the gifts of the community. God is encountered in the pilgrim community that is struggling in its particular historical and cultural circumstance. When the community is stratified into hierarchical classes and fragmented social groupings according to age and sex, married and celibate, we are forced to communicate—or try to communicate—across chasms that separate our experiences and perceptions of the world into which we are trying to bring light and unity. We also find ourselves living in a community that, on one hand, is divided into male or female celibates—who also just happen to have a preponderance of the leadership authority—and, on the other hand, into married and/or single persons who, while having made remarkable progress in reclaiming their authority in the

Church, are still largely relegated to a minor position in its overall structure.

Likewise, while Vatican II has opened excellent possibilities for revamping our sense of community and mission, the Church is still struggling to minister to the world from within a fragmented body. As long as celibate men and women have no choice but to attempt to communicate across chasms that separate their lived experiences and prevent them from learning from and about one another—and thus, ultimately, more about themselves—the proclamation of the promise being fulfilled in our lives will be garbled. We will not truly have encountered the promise as a vital, life-giving reality because our cultural conditioning and religious conventions will have deprived us of a truly redemptive and healing community experience. Our belief will be largely theoretical and abstract, our proclamation irresolute and, possibly, altogether empty.

Neither marriage nor celibacy is truly served in the present situation, nor can we truly become living witnesses to a Gospel that calls us to unity in love, unity that would open our lives to ultimate unity with God, who is himself Love.

The ultimate goal of revelation is to bring about the establishment of the Sovereign One who is Divine Truth, Love and Unity, whose very essence is to be self-revealing through relationships and communication in truth. Such divine self-giving was most clearly manifest in Jesus, who adamantly refused to recognize class and privilege, not only for himself but also for his disciples. It rather obviously follows, then, that receiving the rule of the One who is Love into our lives and manifesting it in our relationships means that our community must be one, bonded in charity and mutually interacting in service, not in legally stylized relationships and functions based on the exercise of power, authority, and prestige.

If we claim to be truly a praying community, open to the ongoing revelation of God as our lives, in relationship, interact and unfold together, then we need to take care that we do not allow obstacles to impede the development of true and free relationships. It is in such interactions—not impeded or distorted by unconscious projections, unrealistic expectations, or legal sanctions—that personal growth in self-knowledge takes place. Interactions provide the arena in which a group of individuals can become transformed into a community that redeems and heals by drawing one another from isolation and estrangement into relationships bonded by mutual and unconditional affirmation and support.

Contrariwise, when we attempt to communicate through a maze of role expectations, labels, or masks of authority and power, we attach contingencies and conditions of fulfillment to one another's acceptance and validation in the community. Thereby, we set up a pseudocommunity in place of a pain-filled, but healing community based on the purification and transformation of Christian love. A kind of cheap redemption—in which safety and security of self-identity is based on class and functional role, power, or authority—is substituted for the redemption of the Cross—in which dying, dying to self, means dying to all that is not true in one's self-understanding.

Community provides opportunity for human interaction and engagement with the whole spectrum of human relationships: male and female, young and old, rich and poor, educated and uneducated, married and unmarried. It provides opportunity to learn new possibilities within oneself, for failure as well as for success. In a true community, one is stretched, challenged, created, and redeemed. The true life of God is revealed as one's false ego-structures are dismantled, as one's fear and defensiveness are exorcised, and as one is allowed to stand and be, transparent and frail, in need of and being needed by the community. Until this becomes not only possible but normal, the world at large will be denied an experience of the true light of Christ's presence in power, now in his Mystical Body.

While I have referred several times to the negative aspects of legalizing human relationships, I do not intend to suggest that the legal structure carries the full burden of responsibility for the present dilemma. That would be altogether too simple and it would cause us to despair of ever being able to bring about change. In fact, the problem can be either dismantled or held intact by our own attitudes. This is chiefly what the Gospel is about: a call to change our attitudes, perceptions, and, ultimately, our relationships. It is our attitudes and perceptions of ourselves and others that put people on pedestals, that project our romantic and idealized self-images onto other persons or classes; thus, we project our infantile needs for superparent onto Mother Church or her representatives. To be a true community means that we accept the responsibility to grow to mature adulthood, to free others from our needs and expectations, and to embrace one another without illusion, each for what we are and are called to become. It does not mean that we do not have roles and functions in the community, but that those roles, with their functions, are the means whereby we are given in service to the community while having our own needs met and ministered to.

To fail to believe in and strive for the maturity and freedom that enable us to free the Church and one another from our projections and expectations is simply to make the Church another idol, an impediment in our path, another obstacle on our way to wholeness and personal union with God. Instead of being "the way" that leads to a personal encounter with a living god, the Church becomes a fortress providing a false sense of security, deceiving the pilgrim into thinking the journey is over, the goal reached. So the pilgrim becomes a settler.

When Peter put himself protectingly in the path of Jesus as he moved toward Jerusalem and the Cross, and as Peter attempted to dissuade Jesus from his goal, Jesus minced no words. "He rebuked Peter and said to him, 'Get behind me, Satan! Because the way you think is not God's way but man's'" (Mk.8.33). The key to dismantling the self-destructive entanglement with our self-serving projections lies within our willingness to surrender attitudes, expectations, unreflective assumptions and values to the purification and transformation outlined in the Gospel, lived and modeled by the apostles and disciples, to exchange our way of thinking for God's as revealed in Jesus Christ. The conversion of the Church begins with our own purification and transformation, which can come about only through silent, attentive presence to God's Word in the deep solitude of our hearts. Contemplative prayer is the openness that allows God's Word to penetrate and enlighten our consciousness, the same penetration and enlightenment that the author of Hebrews speaks of: "The word of God is something alive and active: it cuts like any double-edged sword but more finely: it can slip through the place where the soul is divided from the spirit, or joints from the marrow; it can judge the secret emotions and thoughts. No created thing can hide from him; everything is uncovered and open to the eyes of the one to whom we must give account of ourselves" (Heb.4.12-13).

7

The Solitude of Celibacy

I have pointed out that celibacy is a substantial, living reality existing in individual persons with names and relationships. We cannot speak of it as either a collective community reality or an abstraction unless we keep it related to that fundamental fact. I think that pontiffs and theologians, both past and present, have fallen into error in that respect. The result is that we tend to idealize the state of celibacy and speak of it in the abstract, forgetting that, in reality, it wears the scars and bruises, the configuration of individual lives and relationships. We often bring value judgments to our encounter with the celibate experience because we see it always related to the romanticized version and judged in that light. We find ourselves uncomfortable with the lived reality and tend to become distressed or scandalized when human frailty becomes all too obvious a factor. We want our celibates to be Saran-wrapped and odor-free.

Celibacy lives at the center of life; it affects the personal, subjective experiences of the person, substantively changing the quality of life and relationships. Conversely, the subjective experience of being a person qualitatively determines the way in which celibacy is encountered and made manifest to the world.

While we might like to think and act as if only saints are truly representative of the Church, we are allowed no such fantasy. The Church exists and lives just as much in rascals and ne'er-do-wells as it does in saints. If that were not the case, you and I would most assuredly have no place in her membership. Celibacy must be owned and recognized, not only in saints and mystics but as well in the struggling sinner who seems to have more than his or her share of human weakness. Celibacy lives and is realized in our ability to rebound, to continue hoping in what is possible, to keep the victory of Christ in our vision, and to continue believing in ultimate victory, not the victory of our own white-knuckled efforts, but the victory of God's mercy.

The celibate person lives in relationships. The quality of celibacy at any given time will reflect the quality of community. If the community is judgmental, condemnatory, damning, and fragmented, then the celibate person who does not measure up to the standards of that community will be thrust into alienation and a web of guilt that exacerbates and intensifies the problem, rather than healing it and redeeming the victim. When the community realistically accepts individuals in its midst and recognizes a common dependence on the healing mercy of Christ and a mutual responsibility to mediate that healing and forgiveness, then celibacy—like matrimony—will become the sign of Christ's presence that it was meant to be.

Whatever we might say about celibacy, we celibates need to begin to realistically experience the celibate reality in the actual here-and-now condition of our individual humanity. That is the starting point of our growth into mature, happy, well-adjusted members of the Body of Christ. We cannot hope to achieve happiness and growth if we begin by measuring ourselves against some abstract ideal of romanticized heroes or heroines. Celibacy lives and will grow as a positive, life-giving experience for me when I accept the fact that my unique experience as a person is the seedbed from which this community charism will grow and achieve its presence in the community. However celibacy might function in the community, it will bear the marks of my individual humanity, seeking to grow into union with God, who is Love.

Celibacy is a choice to not marry, to not satisfy the deepest longing of the human heart to give love and receive it back in an intimate and exclusive manner. Since it entails a decision to not bear children who will carry one's lineage beyond this lifetime into new possibilities in the future, is celibacy a dead end? Is it the ultimate self-annihilation? Can we, through celibacy, give witness to the goodness of humanity and creation and proclaim our abiding belief in the promise contained within human life? In short, can we, barren on one level of life, become fruitful for humanity? That is the question and the challenge, as well as the hope, that must live at the center of a celibate life.

Celibacy leaves an empty space, a void, that demands attention. It is by attention to the empty space, this place of unfilled longing, that we are led to the highest possible fulfillment of human maturity. Conversely, it is by ignoring the space or anesthetizing it that we are left in the shallows of human relationships. The frustration of the tantalizing elusiveness of human accomplishments become monuments to the emptiness and futility of lives seeking to be filled and satisfied with mere shadows of reality.

Residing in a person created for and struggling to find unity and meaning in relationships with others, celibacy, by its nature, places the person in a state of contradiction. It plunges him or her uncompromisingly into the depth of solitude, with a sense of being mortal, yet apart and alone, facing the possibility of extinction. From that sense emerges a fear of nonbeing, with the consequent felt need to make one's life count, or to leave one's mark on history. That is not theology or poetry. It is hard reality that cannot be poeticized or theologized away. An option for celibacy is an option to live one's life in the midst of the solitude of human longing for love and unity with another. Unless that solitude is absorbed by the power of a living faith towards union with the God of all life, it will be subject to seduction by faith in lesser gods. The solitude of existence cannot be put off. It demands to be addressed and nourished by normal and legitimate human love and intimacy, which draws it beyond its egotistical self to life-giving union with another. In such a union, God is discovered as divine love commingling with human love, purifying it, and drawing it into final union with him in charity. That is why marriage is the ancient symbol of the relationship between God and his people.

The celibate person, deprived of that union by choice, law, or nature, needs to beware of the deception of thinking that celibacy is accomplished by simply keeping it on a volitional and logical level, surrounded and supported by cultural and religious conventions. If the celibate is not consciously living on the forward edge of a developing faith and union with God, pseudogods will soon move into the emptiness of unrequited solitude. All too soon the fruits become evident in self-indulgent behaviour, eccentric isolation, inappropriate withdrawal from healthy social relationships, disproportionate interest in material possessions, sensual pleasures and gratifications. It is as if the psyche were frantically driving one to fill the space with personal immortality projects before it is time for the soul to plunge into oblivion. Unrequited solitude drives us on a futile search for unity and immortality, for which the human heart was created and which only the infinite God can satisfy.

With the celibate option comes the decision to live one's life from within the depth of personal solitude, shared with all humanity, through which one becomes drawn into God's own divine life. Thus, celibacy is a choice for living in unmediated union with the God of Life. It is a choice to embrace, in one's own solitary existence, the solitude and longing of all humanity for the realization of final unity with the Beginning and the End, the One in whose image each of us was created.

In celibacy, prayer can never be segmented into time and place, for celibacy is the continual self-giving of one's life from within the actual condition of that life at any given moment. Celibacy, prayer, and life are as inextricably linked as air, water, and life. One who is truly living celibacy will be drawn into prayer naturally, "as a doe longs for running streams" (Ps. 42.1). Likewise, to truly seek prayer in a deep and personal way, to focus life on the centrality of prayer as an encounter with God at the center of one's being, will transform the solitary center of life into the meeting place with the God of all life. Through living union with God, the solitary celibate enters into a union with all creation, with all life, with every person. It is a union that more generously, more freely, more truly involves him or her in an encounter with the human predicament. In short, it humanizes. True solitude is not really withdrawal, rejection, or escape from those with whom we share life; rather, it is a process of rooting our lives and relationships at the center of our own "unique-beingness," where the terrible aloneness of our solitude is intersected by and becomes one with the oneness of God, in whose divine life we participate and which we share with all created beings.

When the celibate option is rooted in the solitary center where our lives and God's life intersect and become one, we are able to enter into fully human, fully redemptive relationships with humanity and created things, because in this union we have all and want nothing. We can allow creation—other persons—to be what they are capable of being without laying demands on them. The projections, expectations, and egotistical demands placed upon things or persons in my life have been laid to rest. I can allow others to be truly who they are and can accompany them on their journey to maturity in freedom, without my own ego-needs and expectations getting in the way.

True community, true belonging—with its self-giving as well as receiving—is the fruit of a balanced rhythm between solitude on the one hand and communal presence and action on the other. Without such balance and rhythm, efforts to be a community of witness and service can become entangled in unconscious agendas and conscious "relationalizations," manipulations, and defensiveness. The process of entering into that balance is by no means easy. The fact is that there is no easy, cheap way to attain true unity and ministry. Christ waits to be born in each of us. To allow his divine life to be one with our lives, there is no way but the way of the Cross, the way to light and truth that leads through all that is not light. To follow that way is to encounter and name all that is dark and untrue, all that is hypocritical and shallow in our lives and relationships.

As prayer leads to the solitary center of the celibate's being, and as the solitude of life is more boldly and courageously encountered and embraced, the egotistical deceptions of false unity, false security, and false relationships are dismantled to reveal the ultimate and final celibate option: to surrender to the terrible oneness of the God of infinite mystery, the unknown and unknowable God of infinite possibility. Francis Thompson has said it all as I believe no other person has said it before or since. His words eloquently reflect the excruciating pain as well as the ecstacy of the purifying process.

> Now of that long pursuit
> Comes on at hand the bruit;
> That Voice is round me like a bursting sea:
> "And is thy earth so marred,
> Shattered in shard on shard?
> Lo, all things fly thee, for thou fliest Me!
> Strange, piteous, futile thing,
> Wherefore should any set thee love apart?
> Seeing none but I makes much of naught" (He said),
> "And human love needs human meriting,
> How has thou merited—Of all man's clotted clay the dingiest clot?
> Alack, thou knowest not
> How little worthy of any love thou art!
> Whom wilt thou find to love ignoble thee
> Save Me, save only Me?
> All of which I took from thee I did but take,
> Not for thy harms,
> But just that thou might'st seek it in My arms.
> All which thy child's mistake
> Fancies as lost, I have stored for thee at home;
> Rise, clasp My hand, and come!"
> Halts by me that footfall;
> Is my gloom, after all,
> Shade of His hand, outstretched caressingly?
> "Ah, fondest, blindest, weakest,

I am He whom thou seekest!
Thou dravest love from thee, who dravest Me."

(Francis Thompson. "The Hound of Heaven." *Poetry of the Victorian Period.* 3rd ed. Comp. Jerome H. Buckley and George Woods. Glenview: Scott, Foresman and Company, 1965).

A call to celibacy is a call to a life of prayer and intimacy with the One. From the beginning, the celibate person needs to recognize and accept that call as a call to prayerful contemplation of and response to the exclusivity of union with the One who is Love over all human life and action. Such was the mystery underlying God's call to Abraham and Sarah, to Moses and the Israelites, to the prophets, saints, and mystics down through the ages of the Hebrew Scriptures. In the Christian covenant, Jesus Christ stands as the One in whom the radical claim of the rule of love draws us into a relationship in which there is no room for anything less than total self-giving, even to death by crucifixion.

Unless the celibate state becomes the way that opens to voluntary acceptance of solitude, poverty, and nonviolence, it can become a treacherous pit of self-deception, all too easily filled with self-serving activities and personal idols. Unfortunately for the spiritual climate of the Church—as well as for the quality of life of the celibate person—prayer, devotion, piety, and faith in general have often been reduced to ritualistic formulas bordering on the magical and superstitious or, at best, to mere sociocultural conventions. This trend has had a deadening effect on many celibates who have wrongheadedly attempted to envelop their celibate state in a network of conformity and propriety, living up to cultural expectations while entirely ignoring personal inner development and growth. Fortunately, in the recent past—since Vatican II dismantled many of our cultural idols—we are experiencing an awakening in the areas of prayer and solitude in healthy tension with human interaction, as well as a healthy asceticism in our personal spiritual lives. There are growing numbers of robust, mature Christians who seek to grow beyond outmoded forms of the past to a free and responsible adulthood in their religious practices and beliefs. They have laid aside the lie that contemplation, the mystical consciousness, is reserved for a chosen, select few.

It is now possible to hope that we will see a rekindling of the gift of celibacy as a sign of hope and promise in the midst of the church community. I do not intend to suggest that this will happen first or foremost, even at all, in the priesthood. As long as seminaries and religious formation programs continue to address the problem by pouring new wine into old wineskins, the future will be bleak. The renewal of the celibate charism cannot be determined by bureaucratic maneuvers or lofty exhortations. Neither can the reawakening of living celibacy be determined by institutional mandate. What is needed is recognition that celibacy lives and grows, rooted in contemplation and personal options. With grounding in contemplative prayer will come the emergence of an awakened mystical consciousness that has its being in an awareness of God, present and active at the center of our lives. The solitude and poverty of celibacy will become the empty space wherein the divine life, the divine energy of love, enters, purifies, and transforms us at the heart of our existence.

Celibacy, in and of itself, is not a good; it is, in fact, highly questionable as a state of life. The only way in which celibacy can be considered a positive good is that it leaves one available to be purified, emptied, and drawn into unity with the divine energy of love. Contemplation is the process through which the celibate person brings himself or herself into an attentive, waiting, listening encounter with the Word of God. An intellectual, cognitive, rational encounter will not do.

God's Word is living. It reveals and makes known the innermost mystery of our true selves. It exposes and calls to judgment the falsity and delusion of our lives, relationships, and actions (Heb. 4.12-13). It opens the way to simplicity, truth, and poverty of spirit; it puts the gentleness of nonviolence in place of the unredeemed values of emotional, sexual exploitation that rule our society; it brings to birth the life of Christ in us and draws our minds and hearts from the shadows of sin into the mind and heart of Christ. A life of contemplative presence to God's Word is the only right option for the celibate, for, unless celibacy leaves us empty, poor, and vulnerable to God's Word, we are open and available to the deceptions of our own egocentric desires and needs. Succumbing to the seduction of that vulnerability is manifest by the frantic need to do and to accomplish; to be esteemed and affirmed by the conventions of our culture, those very conventions we are called to stand against. The void of celibacy is co-opted by the fear of being alone, standing on the brink of personal oblivion. Celibacy then is a sin and a scandal. Instead of being a sign of contradiction, a sign of the promise, instead of being the way to full life in God, celibacy becomes the way to darkness and spiritual death for oneself and, very possibly, for others.

Words such as *solitude, contemplation, mysticism, and holiness* undoubtedly conjure up thoughts and images of strange, extremist kinds of persons, places, and activities—any place but our normal, everyday environment with its activities; any time but the workday, which is all day from the time we get up in the morning until bedtime; any person but me, burdened as I am by a sense of sinfulness and inadequacy. We are reluctant to believe that our own prayer, our life with the Lord, can ever be anything but basic repetition of routine formulas and faithful adherence to law and custom. For many of us, spiritual life consists of grim, muscle-bound efforts to get through the day without bungling something too badly, and if, in the process, we can manage to perform one or two generous acts or resist one or two temptations, we are to be congratulated. Too many of us have become resigned to living in the shallows of folk piety and conventional religious devotion that have little connection with the heroic and awesome potential contained within the human person and challenged to come forth in the chronicle of salvation history.

If we delve beneath the surface of words and imagery in Sacred Scripture, we will become aware that God reveals himself as one who enters into the course of human history, through human beings, in order to draw the human race from darkness to light and, through human mediation, to establish proper and true relationships in creation and in the human family. That, in brief, is what redemption and holiness are really all about. In effect, it is what the practices, disciplines, and laws of organized religion are all about. They allow human consciousness the time and the environment, the stillness, in which to hear God's Word calling us to change, to leave our captivity and move into that place, that attitude of mind and heart in which God's truth, his law, can lay claim to all of our actions and relationships in order that he might lead us to truth.

A relationship with God is dynamic; it is process, growth, development, and transformation. In theological language, it is a call that, if heard and responded to, must necessarily bring change, even radical change. Abraham and Sarah were obliged to get up and leave, even when they had no clear idea of where they were going. Following God's call cannot always be reduced to rational, logical formulas with airtight guarantees. Abraham and Sarah, as well as the Israelite community in the Exodus experience, put their lives in jeopardy and submitted themselves to the purifying action of God, whose wisdom went beyond theirs. As a result, they did not always understand what was happening until long after the event had occurred. So, too, the contemplative process entails a docile, obedient heart that is open to trust. It is grounded in the belief that God is good, true, faithful, and holy; that he desires to lead us to our own truth, fidelity, and holiness through the union of our lives with his. Before that union can occur, we must be purified from all that is not true and holy. We must be freed from the tyranny of human logic, the constricted dimension of our reason; from the burden of needing to know, to be sure; in short, from the delusion of control. Those are the demons of modern religion that cause many of us to become entangled in self-righteousness and arrogant hostility towards others who believe and behave differently than we do. Under such influence, religion falls into the trap of the control and power of authority. The tidiness of the conventional thinking and self-serving values of organized religion becomes more dangerous than no religion at all, because it deceives us into thinking that we have solved the ultimate mysteries of life.

We are dealing with the same demons that ultimately thwarted the salvific power of Christ, for he could not save those who had already saved themselves with their ironclad legalism and mindless ritualism. Christ could not penetrate the security system of those who had surrendered themselves to the cheap salvation promised by a religious system that promoted salvation through the unquestioning observance of human law and tradition. Celibates and the professional religionists of our day need to courageously confront those demons, those occupational hazards of our vocation to see if, possibly, we have been duped into the same sort of arrogance of the heart, precluding the possibility of opening to new potential.

All too often today, religious communities and seminaries invite young people into their houses and then, rather than challenging them and calling them beyond the conventional values of their culture, lead them into an unreflective, uncritical affirmation of all that is most deadening and in need of redemption in that culture. The older generation simply passes along and perpetuates what has come to be little more than "American Civil Religion." The materialistic, self-serving arrogance of a culture that feeds off hedonistic impulses becomes enshrined as the supreme value for which we are willing to fight and die, to say nothing of kill. And, while we intensify and increase our prayers for vocations, we wonder why celibacy and the Evangelical Counsels fail to stimulate the idealism of the young. We tend not to realize that any religion is a false religion if it does not lead us into a personal, unique relationship with the God of Abraham and Sarah, if it does not stretch us beyond our socioreligious bondage, our culturally defined frontiers, roles, and functions.

Priests, religious, laity—all of us need to confront the reality of our day and recognize that all too often we are struggling with a fossilized remnant of what once was a dynamnic and life-giving challenge to humanity. True religion challenges us to reach beyond our limited self-understanding so as to touch the transcendent dimensions of our humanity. Beginning with the Hebrew Scriptures and continuing through the Book of Revelation, God affirms the potentiality of the human person for holiness in love, for participation in a nonjudgmental community living in peace and nonviolence—a community that extends beyond our egocentric selves to our neighbor and beyond, even to the farthest and deepest reaches of creation. He calls us and challenges us to live in a bold confrontation with everything that impedes and limits the expansion of our consciousness toward an awareness of the unity of all things and, through all things, to oneness in him.

Thus, any religion that presents a Christ who does not call us to move beyond culturally defined roles and conventional wisdom to the outer limits of our human potential and to live up to his example of love, justice, compassion, and nonviolence is not worthy of being called Christian. The Cross and the Eucharist remain the archetypal symbols reminding us of who we are and what we are capable of becoming in our relationships with one another and with creation. In those two symbols we find the summation of all that Christ taught and brought about through his Apostles and disciples.

In the fifth chapter of St. Luke's Gospel, we read that having lowered their nets after a futile night of fishing, Peter and his companions caught such a superabundant number of fish that they knew something miraculous had happened. Peter was filled with a bewildering amazement, akin to terror. He fell at Jesus' feet and confessed his sinfulness (Cf. Lk 5. 6-11. *The Amplified Bible*. Zondervan Bible Publishers). After receiving that marvelous sign, the disciples put their boats and nets away and followed him. Their initial gesture of surrender was only the beginning of a long, slow process of intense and painful purification, an emptying and rebirth of the true self that would enable them to reach the deepest recesses of their hearts and awaken others to their own potential for holiness in true freedom and unconditional love. They would be "fishers of men" (Lk 5.10). Their words and actions, their proclamation of the Kingdom would emerge from the center of their true selves, from where self and God intersect and become one, and would reach directly into the hearts of their hearers to awaken, within that solitude, each person's hunger for unity in truth.

Perhaps familiarity with the episode of the draft of fishes has taken the edge off its meaning for us. The fear and amazement that Peter experienced and his confession of sinfulness not only describe his reaction to the episode, but seem also to contain a prophetic intuition of the unfolding process of Peter's relationship to Jesus. Peter had good reason to be filled with bewildering amazement, akin to terror, because, in the normal course of minding his own business, he had been accosted by God's messenger. The Word in unpretentious human flesh, just like his flesh, would now lead Peter and all of the disciples on a course that would leave them devastated and brokenhearted in the collapse of pat little assumptions and limited human expectations.

God's Word had come to Abraham, Sarah, and, through Moses, to the Israelites; each time, it had inaugurated a new epoch in human history. It had led them through excruciating purification and emptying before they could become the instruments of a new creation. In Jesus, God's Word, the same Word of Genesis and Exodus, now in human flesh, continued to bring about a transformation of humanity in which purification and emptying were no less necessary. Through Jesus, Peter found out—as had Moses and Abraham before him—that to encounter God is to encounter a force that can accept nothing less than total and radical truth. To encounter that force is also to encounter all that is not true and holy. To be aware of One's capacity for holiness is also to be aware of all that is not holy in one's life: sin. The first step towards actualizing our capacity for holiness is to accept the revelation of our sin, not deny it. To encounter and accept Jesus Christ is to accept the excruciatingly painful but glorious and liberating process of purification and transformation. We cannot have one without the other.

Peter became the "Rock" of the Resurrection Church because, in spite of his noisy bombast, he submitted to a relationship that would purify him of his glib falsification and shallow assurances, so that his true self, that naked and vulnerable self created for the love of God, became one with God's own life. In Peter the Rock we have the story of a personality reborn in the life of Christ, a new life that is not really new at all, but a restoration of the truth of human creation in God's image. Peter was freed from the tyranny of the sin that had blinded his heart to the truth of itself, that is, its potential for freedom and love. But first he was obliged to travel the frightening path of self-knowledge that included knowledge and acceptance of the tyranny of sin in his life and his relationships.

As Jesus died in truth, allowing God's love to pass through his suffering into a world that rejected him, Peter—and, with him, the infant Church, the mystical Body of Christ—died in shame to all that was not true, not love, not gentleness or forgiveness. Peter was emptied in order to make room for the Holy Spirit of Christ that was poured into the Mystical Body. Peter's death and resurrection to new life in Christ is the image, the paradigm for our life in Christ. It is the paradigm for all Christian prayer and worship.

The listening, waiting stance of a person who, in prayer and solitude, is willing to be vulnerable before God is risky. In the ultimate poverty of spirit, having tasted the futility of everything that holds life together, that person is now ready to put it all in jeopardy. The poverty of spirit is that which, in the marvelous imagery of the "Hound of Heaven" recognizes that "none but I [God] makes much of naught," and then surrenders that "naught" for the creative process. At risk are the assumptions, the certitudes, and the empty promises that have had their origins in our fear of death, of oblivion, of the ultimate aloneness that drives us on our search for peace, social affirmation, and the solace of human accomplishments. Thus Peter, the self-assured, blustery but successful businessman who had all of the answers, sensed that in this mysterious person, Jesus, he was encountering the one who would lay bare the reality of his life and expose it for what it was—a fraud. Small wonder that he trembled in his bones as he sought to put distance between himself and the one who would reveal, so uncompromisingly, his dark side.

The story of that little episode between Peter and God's Word, that struggle of a soul momentarily glimpsing the awesome possibility of the restoration of life and relationships to truth in freedom and encountering in Jesus, the Christ, the echo of God's call to truth, is also the story of our struggle with conversion. If we find ourselves wondering why we labor so diligently through the night and have so little to show for it, perhaps we need to ask ourselves if we have truly allowed Jesus, the revelation of our own truth, to lead us through the dismantling of our own agendas, our own egotistical programs of ministry and prayer to encounter God in the depths of our own hearts. God cannot live in a lie. As long as our lives are entangled in the deceit of conventional religious and cultural values and in the shallowness of folk piety, then we will labor in vain and succeed in doing no more than perpetuate our own shallowness.

Unfortunately, too many of us have accepted the conventional lie that would seduce us into believing we are destined to live and die in the shallow backwaters of conformity to conventional religious practice. We have been lured into the web of cheap redemption that promises salvation and happiness as the reward for a lifetime of docile, unthinking repetition of creeds and fossilized rituals, with unthinking observance of cultural norms that require us to deny sin and cover it over with pretense and evasiveness.

At its fundamental level, prayer is that attitude in a moment of time when we lay all before the Lordship of God's Word, surrender to his truth, and become one with the power of love. It is that moment of vulnerability when we allow ourselves to glimpse the audacity of our assumptions and pretensions that seek to reduce the wonderful mystery of all that we can be and all that God is to the level of our own dwarfed perceptions. The terror, the bewildering amazement comes when we realize that the price we pay for living in the truth is to allow our defenses and pretensions to be surrendered in favor of the light and truth of God, in whose image we are created.

Celibacy puts one at the point of no return. The celibate person either moves forward into an ongoing encounter with the God who purifies and transforms, or remains paralyzed, neither daring to follow the call into the darkness that leads to light and truth, nor knowing the intimate union of life-giving love from another person which just as surely leads to transformation and union with the God of Love. And so the person who has chosen not to surrender to the purifying love of another human being, yet is not open to the unmediated consuming love of a living God, dooms himself or herself to life in the arid, lifeless wastes of false gods of his or her own making. Without the readiness and vulnerability to be drawn into the mystery of God's creative action in history that is the fruit of contemplative prayer and mystical union, and likewise deprived of the humanizing and sanctifying interaction of marriage and procreation, the celibate stands as a sorry caricature of the human person, imprisoned in unredeemed solitude.

A celibate person is freed from the taxing and demanding obligations associated with marriage and the raising of children so that he or she may unreservedly be engaged in an exclusive encounter with the author and source of all life. Anything less than being totally engaged in this mystery is as false and deceptive as saying that one can be only partially married, or only partially a parent. Just as marriage and parenthood often disintegrate under the stresses of infidelities of one sort or another, so too, celibacy can succumb to a life in which priorities are disordered and one is unfaithful to the truth of one's commitment.

A celibate person is one who is able to make realities and terms such as repentance and reconciliation, contemplation, mysticism, and union with God relevant and integrated into the fabric of human affairs and endeavors. One who is truly faithful to the celibate process and creatively engaged in the praying of celibate life stands in the presence of the community and testifies to the immanence, accessability, and normalcy of a life of union with God. In that way, and only in that way, does the celibate person become just as truly generative of new life for the world as does the married couple. They stand together in community, bound by a shared vision of the goodness and the potential of the human family to live in godlike relationships.

8

Prophets for a New Age

When God spoke from the burning bush, Moses was presented with an image that did not easily fit into a penchant for controlling the destiny of life. nor did it admit of allowing life to be controlled by circumstances. God was manifest in such a way that if Moses was going to take seriously the offer of a relationship, he would need to change his notion of his own capabilities and limitations, as well as those of the Hebrew people he was going to lead.

The first image Moses encountered was the rather startling sight of a bush on fire but not consumed. Fire is the symbol of the transformation and regeneration of matter that continually passes from one stage of being to another. The first image we have of God, then, is one of transforming change and unending beginnings grounded in sameness.

History reflects unending becoming. It is the chronicle of the evolution of human consciousness, forever unfolding while remaining rooted in its unchanging being. As one generation passes away, leaving its dreams and projects unrealized, the next generation picks up the rhythm and continues the march toward the receding horizon of human potential. Throughout the passage of history, as institutions and peoples have come and gone, there have been individuals who were wringing their hands over the passing of cherished institutions and traditional values. At the same time, there have been others with charismatic power and vision who have seen new possibilities emerging, have seen the promise of new beginnings even as the old forms were passing away. Those pioneers of the future were characterized by their willingness to live in the darkness and unknowing of the emerging promise.

Change is always stressful because it challenges us to leave the security of what is known for the untried and unfamiliar, lying in the future. The accelerated evolutionary process of our day has placed tremendous stress on members of this generation, who recall when the future was a time of promise wherein they could plan on resting from their labors to enjoy comfort and relative security. We thought we knew what we could expect and plan for—and we expected that the world would remain static until we caught up with our dreams of the future. But, as Arthur C. Clarke wryly observed in *The Adventure of Tomorrow,* "The future ain't what it used to be."

In their need to have some security in this life, as well as in the life to come, many have seen the Church as the last custodian of stability and dependability. However, we are no longer allowed such comfort. The Church has changed; she is asking questions about centuries-old beliefs and practices. Traditions and customs that go back countless generations have been discarded. Truly, this is a time of anxiety and perplexity in all areas of life.

If we look at the unfolding of salvation history, we can find a treasure of hope and renewed promise, as well as a guide for the Church and the Christian community, in meeting and engaging with God, who causes everything in history and creation to become. In that process, neither our pet dreams and expectations nor our attachment to the status quo will be reinforced. Rather, we will face the possibility of discovering a need to move into the vanguard of the emerging Church and society, where new forms and styles are already appearing on the horizon. Genuine religious seeking is not for the faint-hearted nor for those who characteristically see religion as a means of conserving and holding onto their own treasured dogmas and values. We, like Abraham, Sarah, Moses, and the Hebrew people, are being called to allow our assumptions—even our religious assumptions—to be brought to judgment.

Perhaps the Sacred Scriptures of our Judeo-Christian tradition need times like these in order to be seen clearly as the startling revelation of the new possibilities they offer. Perhaps, in these times, we can find the creative tension and challenge that might give new meaning and challenge to the state of celibacy.

When Moses asked for clarification of the identity of the Mysterious One addressing him from the burning bush, the answer came back: "I am he who is" (Ex. 3:14). An astonishing statement! Whoever heard of identifying oneself as a verb? And yet, what incredible mystery and adventure is contained in that enigmatic response! The One speaking is saying that its essence is in action, being in becoming. No static noun, this diety. To encounter this God is to encounter the very essence of the being and becoming of the universe. And so, when Moses and, through him, his people opened themselves to the mysterious force that had seen fit to enter into their history by interrupting their slavery, they too found themselves caught up in the mystery of becoming. They lived and found their identity in the process of unfolding, of moving forward into what was not yet known.

They had gone down to Egypt in order to survive the famine, to preserve their lives and insure their place in history. That honest search for the necessities of life had slowly eroded into the static, hopeless situation of socioeconomic and religious slavery. Now they found themselves living in the freedom, possibility, and promise of a pilgrim people knowing only the sovereignty of a God who could not be grasped as a noun, not as an object that could be controlled and understood, but only as a creative, personal, loving force who would draw them into eternal and infinite possibility and promise. As the new covenant relationship developed in the desert during the forty years of wandering, a rather remarkable two-way revelation began to unfold. While the Eternal, Unknown One continued to be disclosed to the Hebrew people, they found that their own unknown possibility and promise became realized. As they continued to encounter that Unknown and Unknowable One, allowing themselves to be led, they discovered that they too participated in mystery; that they too had depths of new potential that came to light and revealed itself, even as the Holy One continued to self-disclose from within the current of their history and the living tissue of their lives.

The very foundation of our Judeo-Christian revelation, then, is this: God and humanity are in a covenant of unending possibility and promise that goes beyond the abstractions of philosophy, theology, ritual, and law. It is not a covenant with a theory that can be grasped and manipulated by the human mind; it can only be experienced as a force, a power that is becoming, and causing to become, through time. God cannot be known or engaged in a moment of time, but only in passage through time in a partnership of creation. The Hebrew people were the living tissue wherein that divine self-revelation took place. Their history was the current into which the eternally Unknown One entered, to become one with the evolutionary process of the world and humanity that was grounded in the eternal becoming of God.

In the Hebrew Scriptures, the Mysterious One who becomes known only in creative, liberating power is never subjected to the audacious presumption of being named and, thereby, controlled and known within the limited horizons of human understanding. The knowledge of the divine presence is only remotely described in terms of lived experience: awe, wonder, and mystery. El Shaddai is not so much a name as it is a description of a meeting with the God of the remote wastes, the God of the mountain wilderness, of places of mystery where the soul is laid bare and stripped of all cultural frames of reference. The word *Yahweh* is thought to be related to an archaic form of the Hebrew verb *qal,* "to be" in the sense of eternal presence—not in a static sense, but as one who accompanies as the ground of all becoming. And so Moses was told that he was experiencing and encountering the same force that was with Abraham, Isaac, and Jacob, a force that would continue to be with him, Moses, in the ongoing becoming of his people. "This is my name for all time, and thus I am to be invoked for all generations to come" (Ex. 3:15). A personal relationship with God, which is what all Judeo-Christian revelation and practice is about, cannot be reduced to analytical categories, legal formulas, or ritualistic practices. The God of Moses is a God who lives; his existence is in the act of being in becoming. God cannot be known, that is, possessed. He can only be engaged in his becoming.

To encounter the living God is to encounter a power that engages and activates our own becoming. A relationship with God is entered into through surrender to the unfolding mystery of creation, of history, and of our lives in relationship to God, who is the source of all. In that process, humanity unfolds into the potential and promise that lies beyond the frontiers of our present perceptions and understanding. We know and are known as we become. And so, in a real sense, we too are shrouded in mystery, for our true self is always more than our present perceptions can apprehend. We are pilgrims passing through the present on our way to full being in the totality of God's being. Like God, we cannot be contained in a given moment or experience. We are led into the mystery of what it means to be human and engaged in the divine enterprise of creation as it, and we, continue through history. (Westman, Heinz. *The Structure of Biblical Myths, The Ontogenesis of the Psyche*. Dallas: Spring Publications, 1983).

Perhaps another way of plumbing the depths of the mystery is to see God as the great Destroyer/Creator. God is the one who extends horizons and shatters the time-bound frontiers of human consciousness. To be covenanted to this God is to be liberated from the mediocrity of cultural conventions and called to realize the fullness of our human potential by following El Shaddai into the remote wastes of the forward edge of history. In union with God we are to be involved in the fulfillment of the divine enterprise, the creation of what can be.

In the prologue of John's Gospel, Jesus is identified as the eternal Word of God who is, in fact, God (Jn. 1:1- 14). Just as the Word entered into the nonbeing of precreation and brought forth everything that exists, so now the eternal creative Word takes on human flesh and brings light to the darkness of human history. Again we see that God revealed himself by participation and action in human affairs, in the ongoing process of drawing creation to completion. The forward thrust of that process, the dying and coming to new life, is a manifestation of the divine presence and power bringing creation into being and sustaining it throughout history.

Christian revelation distinguished a new epoch in which the Divine Word, as one like us in all things but sin, was made available to all who would see and hear. The Resurrection event marked the time when the Christian community received the divine inpouring of the Holy Spirit, taking on the configuration of human flesh and drawing humanity into the likeness of Christ—his Mystical Body—in history. History and society were poised on the threshold of transformation through Jesus Christ, and after the Resurrection, through his Mystical Body, Jesus became the enlightening presence in creation and history, continuing to bring light to darkness and order to chaos. He challenges us with what is still possible in human life. He leads the way to the fulfillment of human promise while leaving us free to follow, or not. Thus, we are brought to a crisis, a moment of decision: whether to yield to the impulse of fear, timidity, and the desire to conserve the status quo or the impulse to participate in ongoing creation by surrendering to the eternal becoming of God, who is the truth of all things made manifest in the Eternal Word, Jesus the Christ.

If divine revelation is seen as God's initiative in entering into the course of creative evolution, and if Jesus Christ is seen as the definitive Word of Truth of what it means to be human within the overall context of the evolutionary plan, then it is plain that Christian revelation places the believer on the forward edge of the emerging future as a living sign of hope in the fulfillment of God's promises.

To see Christianity in that light means that Christian ministry meets God, on one hand, in the empty space between present reality and, on the other, in future reality coming to be in the present. We are the people of El Shaddai, the God of the remote wastes, of the mountain wilderness, who is continually creating and bringing into being. We are the people who live under the sovereignty of his wisdom and truth, intersecting with the historical process through the submission of our consciousness to his revelation. The Christian is one who engages in preparation for the coming of the new without fully knowing what that is. We live, as did Abraham, Sarah, Moses, and the Israelites, in the desert wastes where God continues to cause to be, to create anew, and to open the human consciousness to what is possible.

In the Epistle to the Romans, St. Paul exhorts his listeners to trust in the power of God, who worked his will through Jesus Christ and poured his Spirit upon the earth. We are called to live in that Spirit, who gives new life through Jesus Christ, our Redeemer from the law of sin and death. The Spirit now lives in us and brings us into unity with the Wisdom of God, praying within us and crying out from our hearts, "Abba—Father" (Rom. 8.1-15). The Spirit of God, who is in perfect accord with the mind of God, lives in us and knows our hearts; he waits for our surrender to being led into the fullness of life in God, who is the perfect truth of our lives.

One of the most serious impediments to living a bold and prophetic witness is our reluctance to believe that God trusts and calls us individually to be in union with him and to walk in his power. Ultimately, that is a result of failure to believe in our essential goodness and in his wisdom living in us so as to transcend our self-doubt—our sin—and to live in the freedom of knowing that God's wisdom can be the light of our lives and actions.

Created in God's image, we are endowed with participation in the divine life; therefore, we are capable of God-like actions and relationships grounded in God's justice and the peace of nonviolence. That is the essence of living in union with God, no matter how imperfectly or tentatively; in a union that begins with the acceptance of a personal call to believe that I am loved, affirmed, and anointed by God to make his Word present in my life and actions; in a union that ultimately extends into eternity.

To be willing to be opened to a relationship with the living God is to assent to the crucifixion and death of a life of personal egocentric autonomy and individualism. It is to be freed from the compulsion of needing to defend the delusion of power and control, which is the fantasy of the inflated ego. Dying to that fantasy is being freed to live in the truth of our lives, that truth where our human lives and God's life intersect and become one. To turn loose of the egocentric mask of self-autonomy is to be freed to live in and become one with the eternal and infinite being and becoming of God-With-Us. Such was the mystery of the power that was showered upon the Pentecost community.

Recall, as I observed earlier, that the Pentecost community was a brokenhearted, shattered, disillusioned group of people. They had encountered the Destroyer/Creator, who had seen through the darkness of their egocentric identities. In contrast to them, Jesus, the perfect image of the Father, was, at the same time, the perfect image of the truth of humanity—the new Adam—the fullest actualization of humanity. As such, he could not abide settling for a lie. He gently, firmly, and resolutely led the disciples to the Cross—to the death of the untruth in their lives—and left them there, emptied and in the ruins of their own delusions. It was into those ruins that the Spirit of the Risen Jesus was poured in order to bring forth the new age through a transformed humanity, the age of the temple built of living human flesh, purified and made ready to be the Body of Christ.

The Church of Christ lives in the tension between the Cross and the Resurrection: always dying, always rising to new life. It is continually dying because there is no end to possibilities for new life that can never be entered into until we move from what we know into what we do not yet fully know. Only the pilgrim enters the Kingdom.

Luke, in Acts 10, gives us an image of the continuing growth of the Christian consciousness, growth that leads to a deeper understanding of the implications of the Christ-event for the world beyond the Jewish community. In order for that growth to take place in Peter and the Apostles, it was necessary that they relinquish the notion of ritual purity regarding food and personal associations with Gentiles. Doing it was a bold and courageous decision that put Peter in direct confrontation with accepted religious convention.

We need to appreciate how deeply ingrained were ritual laws in the hearts of the Jewish people before we can grasp the significance of the growth that took place in the community of believers. When Peter saw the vision of the sheet, full of unclean animals, being let down from heaven, he was shocked and indignant at the command: "Now, Peter; kill and eat!" His startled response, "Certainly not, Lord; I have never yet eaten anything profane or unclean" (Acts 10. 14-15) created a moment of high drama in the growth of Christian consciousness. Peter was to be the channel that would lead the Christian community beyond the boundaries of ritual sectarianism to become a Church that would embrace the ends of the earth and penetrate all cultures and every human heart. As the vision unfolded, Peter's heart was freed from its deep bias as God revealed to him that the new covenant is one to be given to all nations and all peoples. The new covenant is catholic in the full meaning of that word; it cannot be circumscribed by cultic law and ritual, nor can any one religious system claim to have the last word as to who or how one encounters the Saviour.

Peter's developing consciousness and understanding of the new possibilities under the guidance of the Holy Spirit enabled him to put the old law into perspective; a new revelation was replacing the old, but that required bold and courageous mediation. It called forth from Peter a new sense of his own role in the divine plan. For him to be an Apostle and to proclaim the Gospel, he needed to continue to be opened to the new and to let go of the old.

So it was with every aspect of life in the early community. Time, suffering, patience, and courage were needed for the Church to plumb the depths of the mystery that, through Jesus Christ, had changed the course of history and was now being carried through history in that community. To Paul, Barnabas, Peter, and James fell the task of dealing with the issue of circumscision and the reluctance of some to dispense with the law of Moses (Acts 15). They were the mediators of the power of God's Spirit doing a totally new thing, creating a new current that would carry them in a totally new direction, unpredictable and unthinkable to any but those whose minds and hearts had been touched and opened by the fire, wind, and earthquake of Pentecost.

Luke's Gospel provides for us a clear example of how the salvific plan of God is a partnership between God's holy wisdom and the free will of humanity. God depends on human mediation to embody his wisdom and carry it to fruition, to make his will done on earth as it is in heaven. United with God's Holy Spirit, the human spirit is enlarged with bold vision and courage to confront the obstacles and impediments to bringing about the reign of the Kingdom.

It remains for persons of faith to make a decision to leave the fragile security of their power to control and conserve, and to step into an engagement with the unknown God of Mystery, who can only be apprehended in the experience of becoming. God, as revealed to us in Sacred Scripture, cannot be engaged in the neat formulas of temple ritual. Only in the action of our lives, in the unfolding history of creation, can we encounter and become one with the divine energy of love that is drawing all things to unity (Phil. 2:9-11, Col. 1:15-20).

Here is where the celibate person finds power and life to fill the void that is the solitude of celibacy. To follow God in the redemption of the historical process is a bold and courageous assent in faith to the promise of God and the summons of Christ.

The state of celibacy, embraced from the standpoint of the Kingdom, leaves one with the freedom to live a prophetic and evangelical life, manifesting and proclaiming the Good News of the conquest of sin and death and the return of history to the sovereign rule of God's wisdom. Celibacy leaves one free to give dramatic witness to the unfolding of the kingdom of God through the historical evolutionary process by boldly engaging in the redemption of history. In that freedom, one can make a radical commitment to the Evangelical Counsels as put forth in the Sermon on the Mount (Matt. 5-7).

The celibate person is freed from the constraints that fall, by necessity, on those who have assumed the responsibility of providing for a family. The celibate person steps aside from the contemporary flow of culture and proceeds on the way to new possibilities, grounded in the Evangelical Counsels. The radical nature of the Gospel can find clear articulation in a life of uncompromising simplicity, focused on the root values of the Gospel. Thus celibacy can provide the freedom to boldly proclaim the truth of the Gospel—the goodness, the promise, and the holiness of the historical process, infused with the light of Christ.

A person living in the freedom of celibacy has the option of standing against the forces of egocentric conservatism as well as egocentric liberalism, both of which are grounded in fear and the fruits of that fear, the need to control. If a celibate is strengthened by a relationship with the God who creates history, fear is robbed of its power. One who has nothing to lose or to gain is free to surrender to the hope that is rooted in the promises of God, made to his people and fulfilled throughout the generations down to our own time. The person living the mystery of celibacy is blessed with the freedom to live on the forward edge of the historical process.

If a celibate person is drawn by the promise of the sanctification of history and creation and by a sense of the cosmic proportions of the Resurrection-Ascension-Pentecost event, then he or she may prophetically enter into the forward thrust of history, anchored in the tradition of our spiritual Fathers and Mothers; they have kept alive the promise in order to hand it on to us who, in their present, were the unknown future.

If, in faith, we peer into the imagery of Sacred Scripture and tradition, we see that the Judeo-Christian world view is based on trust in the essential goodness of creation, the capacity of the human person to live a godly life in right relationships—not only with our human family, but with nature, creation, and history, as well.

In the Gospel according to Luke, between the account of Jesus' baptism in the Jordan and that of his temptation in the desert, the author inserted an extensive geneology that takes the lineage of Jesus all the way back to Adam, son of God, created in His image and given the task of guiding the creative process (Lk. 3. 23-38). By linking Jesus to the history of humankind, Luke was signifying that Jesus incorporates, recapitulates, and brings to fulfillment in his life the totality of human history—the good with the bad, the promise present and active even in darkness and human failure. In his life, like ours in all things but sin, history was baptized and brought into the desert to be tempted, to confront the evil that tyrannizes the human heart, and to be taken to new possibilities that ultimately lead to the Cross of unconditional love and nonviolence. The Cross is the sign of ultimate possibility for the human family to hope and believe in its capacity to progress beyond violence and greed to nonviolence and love. That is the ultimate direction of all history.

The only truly Judeo-Christian attitude toward the created world and the historical process is that it is the same ongoing evolutionary process that began with the sending of the Word into the darkness and chaos of pre-creation (Gen.1). The Word sent into the darkness and chaos of human history in the person of Jesus Christ is the same Word continually unfolding, "causing to become" in our own time. Indeed, the constant theme throughout Hebrew-Christian Scripture is that the evolutionary process, the current of human history, is a divine-human enterprise ultimately leading to an absolute and final unity with the Divine in love. Sin enters and thwarts the enterprise when human beings forget the reciprocity of their relationship with God, the human family, and material creation. Thus a sense of mutuality, of community, is displaced by suspicion, fear, and egodefensiveness. Such a negative attitude manifests itself in the historical process by seeing change, transformation, the future as personally threatening to our hard-earned security. Out of fear, we strive to conserve and hold fast to sacred and profane dogmas and rituals by idolizing them and imparting to them absolute and unquestioned value. So the historical process becomes fragmented, deprived of its true light, Divine Wisdom, imparted by a living gospel, incarnate in the community of believers.

That is the point at which contemplation and action converge and become one reality, present in one person. Contemplation is the process whereby our consciousness becomes infused with the light of God's truth. The Gospel takes on flesh and continues to spread its light through our lives, not in the knowing of the intellect, but in the flesh of our hearts, our emotions, and wills, thereby transforming our relationships and actions. Such transformation begins with a new understanding of our own person-hood, an acceptance of the eternal destiny of our lives, rooted in the eternal life and truth of God. The boundaries that limit our perceptions of reality gradually dissolve and allow us to perceive all things as bound together in the unity of God. From this renewed perception, our lives in transformed relationships become our ministry. We are not as much concerned with what we are doing, or how much we are doing, as with the quality of our presence and our awareness in the least significant of our actions.

In the charism of celibacy, lived in faith and hope, the Church has enormous power for witnessing to the radical nature of the Gospel. Through the celibate presence, the Church has resources at her disposal to proclaim, in unambiguous language, the sovereignty of God's Word over history and the evolutionary process of human consciousness and understanding. The celibate who remains unmarried for the sake of the Kingdom stakes everything on his or her belief that the present moment is already unfolding into fulfillment of the promise for which the heart of humanity—and of all creation—hopes,even without knowing it. Essentially this means that the celibate finds identity, generativity, meaning, and purpose in the prophetic stance that faces the future and all that it holds. Through the celibate presence, the Church can find the boldness, the courage, the fearlessness that has enabled her to stand against the tides of darkness, of sin, and of fear so as to redirect the divine-human enterprise towards its rightful end: the rediscovery of the true potential of the human person for truth, freedom, and nonviolence under the sovereignty of the Lord of All Creation.

Afterword

The Challenge of Freedom

An essential of any religious experience is reverence, a quality of the human spirit that enables us to discern mystery unfolding and to perceive realities lying beyond our sensible perceptions waiting to be realized. Reverential awe is grounded in the belief that the object of our reverence has a depth that can be realized only when it is free to live out its mystery in a continuing process of self-revelation.

When our relationship with someone or something is tainted by fear and insecurity, we confuse our perceptions of the object for the total reality. Whenever we are prompted by fear, there can be no reverence and the freeing power of love is stymied. There is no room for mystery or surprise. We cling to and control the object of our love, lest we lose the delusion of possession. Our relationship is based on a figment of our imagination, rather than on the reality. As the object of our love reveals itself in all its facets and possibilities, so our projections are withdrawn, our delusions diminished, and our love rooted in the truth of the object. But we have difficulty recognizing and accepting the paradox that the more love grows, the more our reverence allows for a free and trusting relationship. True love drives away fear and opens our hearts to loving reverence. In such reverence we find the freedom of a mature relationship that allows the other to live and grow in mystery, to reveal itself to us, to amaze and astonish us with its continually unfolding beauty and its tenacious will to live and prosper. This kind of vulnerability exposes us to the risk of loss and disillusionment even as it makes possible a deeper and more true relationship. The inescapable paradox of authentic human growth and development entails walking the perilous path between loss and gain.

Considering celibacy in this light, we are confronted with some challenging questions. Does our official, bureaucratic relationship with the gift of celibacy truly reflect an attitude of trust and reverence, a belief in the truth and integrity of celibacy as a living gift, given to persons and communities through the power of God's Holy Spirit? Does our present institutional policy manifest a belief and trust in the integrity and personal responsibility of those whom the Church calls to minister to her people as celibate priests? Put more simply, can we discern love, respect, and reverence for an individual's own responsibility in the legal policies surrounding the gift of celibacy?

The church community enjoys and receives the benefits flowing from the gifts of both celibacy and marriage as they reside in and are experienced by individuals in a given set of subjective and objective circumstances. Celibacy is nourished, enhanced, and drawn to its fullest expression only when there is reciprocal, affirmative interaction between the individual and the community. Community is represented by institutional structures which, in turn, are secondary and transitional means whereby shared values are maintained and expressed. One way to gauge the validity of a given set of structures is to assess the efficiency and directness with which they represent and communicate values to be passed on. So it is that in the Church of today we must also ask whether ecclesial structures reflect an attitude of reverence and trust for the integrity of the gift of celibacy as a living, self-revealing thing? Or do they reflect an attitude of fear and suspicion?

The condition of our individual and communal experience of celibacy at a given time or place in the Church provides a clue to the quality of institutional representation of shared values and to the interaction of celibate religious and clergy with the larger Church community. If today we often see and experience the celibate presence in the Church as, at least, uninspiring and possibly even irrelevant or perplexing, we would do well to examine the entire social and psychological network, as well as the legal and bureaucratic elements in which celibacy is experienced.

Compassion and justice, as well as hardheaded reality, prompt us to courageously evaluate our unreflective assumptions and the bureaucratic structures in which these assumptions are imbedded.

We cannot afford the self-serving belief that a person's effort to realize celibacy as a truly generative and positive influence in his or her life, as well as in the life of the community, is strictly a private and solitary enterprise to be shared only with a confessor, a spiritual director, or, possibly, a psychoanalyst. Most especially in the event that the person's inner psychological and spiritual resources become depleted or broken down, we need to examine the social and communal network of relationships in which that person lived and experienced the celibate state.

If, during the lifetime of a celibate priest or religious, that person acquires a relationship with his or her inner life of feelings and intuition, he or she will develop a mature and harmonious sense of unity with the reality of the celibate state. Celibacy will become a true expression of the person's sense of mission to the larger community. It will be congruent with his or her sense of identity and, therefore, will be a statement of understanding of the true meaning of his or her life and place in the human family. Thus, in the solitude of celibacy, one is able to be grounded in the universal human experience and, out of that experience, to enter into and minister to others in the perplexity and mystery of their personal solitude. That does not exclude the possibility of the continuing pain of loneliness, trial, and failure, but those realities can be embraced in a faith conviction grounded in the hope of a redeeming God who draws our human experiences together into a unity with the Eucharistic prayer of Jesus.

Because each human life is essentially a unique, unfolding mystery that cannot be contained, controlled, or predicted without danger of doing serious harm to its unique nature, communal structures and corresponding legal systems must be formed and administered with reverence for and sensitivity to the primordial value of the integrity of the person and of the peculiar combination of gifts making up his or her personality. That includes a recognition of and respect for the person's primary obligation to be obedient to the unfolding truth of his or her life which is, before all else, a unique expression of the Image of God.

It is in the area of respect for one's freedom to respond to the thrust for personal growth and development that we have what I believe to be the greatest challenge to the compassion of the Church. That challenge demands understanding and reverence for the sovereignty of one's proprietorship over personal choices and responsible giving of self to the emerging options coming from one's encounter with life.

Before the Second Vatican Council, when religious women and religious men who were not priests were allowed to request dispensation from their vows, the reason for granting the dispensation was the recognition that to require someone to continue in a life that had become onerous would be counterproductive and harmful to the common good.

During this same period, priests literally had no recourse whatsoever. No option was open to them save that of apostasy, a complete and all but irreversible cutting away from the Church and slipping into the shadows, in many cases to be consumed by guilt and resentment and, if cultural conditioning had its desired effect, to be tormented by fears of final damnation.

I have little doubt that the inflexability of the legal structures, along with the presence of cultural traditions surrounding the religious life and the priesthood, were effective and efficient in determining the decision of many to remain and give themselves over to living out their earlier choice in a life of generous service and growth in personal integrity. But, likewise I think that honesty and logical consistency force us to conclude that many remained simply because they could not muster up the energy to confront and withstand the legal and cultural sanctions. They had been reduced to a spiritual and psychological "coma" where they were simply incapable of taking charge, of being responsible before God and their consciences for the quality of their lives and relationships. How many and who they were could be known only in the privacy of their own hearts.

Perhaps some of the most valuable experiences coming as an aftermath of Vatican II concerned celibacy, religious life, and ministry and were the ones we least expected or wanted. Three of them are strikingly clear. First, with the dismantling and reorganization of non-clerical religious life of women and of men celibacy remained a primary value. As the religious women and men emerged into a more heterogeneous social and religious environment, without the protection of previous safeguards, they were compelled to take stock of the quality of their past decisions and either make fresh choices or renew old commitments based on new self-knowledge acquired under new circumstances and with a whole range of new options. It was within the context of the field of possible new options that many were able to courageously reflect, evaluate, challenge, and then renew their primary commitment to a celibate life in the midst of their modern world. As the gift of celibacy was offered to them under new circumstances, and as they received it and interiorized it as their own, they were able to offer it as gift to those with whom they shared their lives. Celibacy, for many, has become a living reality that speaks of new self-awareness coming out of a new relationship with God, self, and the human family—the fruit of personal responsibility in an environment of freedom.

Likewise, in the upheaval and subsequent confusion following Vatican Council II we can recognize a second enlightening and hopeful development. Many of the most promising and talented members of religious communities chose to return to the lay state. After some period of uncertainty and readjustment following their departure, many, perhaps most, of the religious women and the men who were not priests found their way into productive, reasonably happy and fulfilled lives. In many cases, they continued ministry in a new form by adapting and modifying their orignal ideals to life in the world as spouse and parent or dedicated, unmarried lay person. In most instances, they were received as welcome and valued resource persons in their parish communities. In significant numbers, those persons maintained a dedication to the spirit of the Evangelical Counsels that is an inspiration to their brothers and sisters who remained in their religious communities.

A third unexpected development came from that same dismantling process. As the numbers of religious men and women decreased, ministries that had previously depended on them were found to be facing serious personnel shortages. At the same time, the number of married couples and single persons who were willing and able to step into the breach rose considerably. What happened, in fact, was that the decrease in "religious professionals" created the opportunities needed for lay men and women to respond to the call to ministry, which the highest tradition of the church and the documents of Vatican II insist is the privilege and duty of all by virtue of baptism.

The important lesson here, it seems, is that when we discover within ourselves the freedom to make choices and live the truth of our lives as we come to know it, and when that freedom is encouraged and reinforced by the Church, either actively or passively, new energy is released and made available to the Church community. We have discovered, perhaps to the dismay of many, that celibacy and the vowed life are not essentially related to ministry. Religious communities with defined apostolates cannot claim a monopoly on evangelical zeal, expertise, or a readiness to spend one's life in the service of others. It seems that the celibate option needs to find its validity and fruitfulness, not in the delusion of somehow being spiritually superior, either in holiness or in zeal for service, but in being present in a way that complements the presence of lay married and single persons.

As often happens, there is a darker, more distressing side of the story. During the pontificate of Pope Paul VI, there was a lenient and compassionate attitude towards priests who asked release from active priestly ministry and the obligation to lifelong celibacy. Again we saw most of those men pick up the loose ends and enter into productive, satisfying lives. The tragedy is that even with the leniency and compassion of the reigning pontif, those inactive priests were systematically excluded from every kind of official participation in Church ministry. We had made some progress since the days when they were forced to apostasize, but we still refused to allow them to participate in the life of the Church in any but the most peripheral ways.

In more recent times there has been a subtle retightening of the legal sanctions. Unmistakable signs of that can be seen in demeaning and humiliating bureaucratic proceedures, in delays and silences, as well as in outright refusals, all of which serve to intimidate and wear down the spirit of the person involved.

What does all of this say about our belief in the capacity of the charism of celibacy to live in an environment where free choice is respected and affirmed as a mark of a mature person, ready and willing to take ownership and responsibility for life? What does it say about our belief in the ability of seminaries and formation programs to effectively train young people to interiorize, own, and be responsible for their option to be celibate? And, when one is barred from the service of the altar and ministry to the faithful because he has chosen to marry, what does that say about our attitudes towards marriage, women, and the raising of children?

These questions center around one major issue that faces the Church today: Do we dare to live as a community in the strict and radical Christian meaning of that word? Can we, as an institution circumscribed by laws and traditions, live the radical and uncompromising call to unity and right relationships—in forgiveness, healing, and compassion—to which the model set by Jesus of Nazareth calls us? Can we, as a church community, give witness to our sense of reverence in the presence of the mysterious unfolding of human life under the guidance of the Holy Spirit?

As members of an institution, we will always require laws to help us identify ourselves in society. However, the quality of the life of the Church, throughout its hierarchical structure, will be determined by the quality of our response to live in mutual understanding and support of one another's efforts to live boldly and honestly the truth of our individual lives in Christ. Laws may help us, but they must never impede or limit our journey towards that truth of our individual lives in Christ. Laws can point towards truth, but the law can never make a person honest, nor can it ever take the place of personal responsibility for the quality of one's character. Law was never intended to limit the potential of human development. Each person at baptism is brought into a relationship with Christ that is both personal and communal. The full actualization of the mystery of Christ in a person is the fruit of a reverential interaction between the mystery of God's life in that person and in the larger community. Laws and customs play a major role in that interaction, but laws and customs need to be constantly kept within their proper context of role and function, that is, to bond the community in charity and to further the process of rooting our lives in Christ. Mere external observance of law can never be a substitute for that relationship. Consequently community, law, and custom are in the service of our discernment of God's will in our individual lives in the community.

Celibacy and the vows of religion are intended for the support and enhancement of the fundamental virtue of religion, which is worship, the surrender of one's life to God's rule of love over all life and creation. The primary value is in that fundamental act of religion, not in the vows themselves. If, in the process of ongoing discernment, one comes to realize that the vows of religion as experienced in a given circumstance are not aiding one towards the end for which they are intended, a dispensation should be sought and granted, as it is today for all except ordained priests. We may ask now why the same option, so reasonable and logically sound in the case of nonclerical religious, is not as readily available to priests. Celibacy may enhance and further the virtue of religion in the community and in the individual person who happens to be a priest, but it is not intrinsically linked either to the priesthood or the act of religion. If one who is a priest has conscientiously discerned that the state of celibacy is, in fact, not supportive of the fundamental act of religion, that it may even be counterproductive, why should he not be readily and affirmatively released from the obligation?

Clearly, the attitude of the official Church towards priests seeking dispensation from the obligation of celibacy is sinful and a scandal of enormous proportions to the community of the faithful, as well as to society at large. The total absence of a spirit of compassion and understanding, with total insensitivity to the dignity of persons, their feelings, their pain, spiritual suffering, and frustration, all testify to the primacy of law and the public corporate image over charity and the healing mission of the Church. In the issue of celibacy and the priesthood, the Church finds herself in a terrible contradiction that belies her stated and avowed purpose of reconciliation and healing, the bringing about of right and true relationships. Yet we cannot allow the upper eschelons of Church hierarchy in Rome to accept the full burden of responsibility for this state of affairs while we stand by in helpless distress, abdicating our own responsibility for participation in the situation and for bringing about change. Each of us needs to examine our attitudes and responses to this situation. For when law and custom blunt our sensitivity to the human dilemma by disregarding the highest values of human dignity and responsible freedom of choice, without calling us to our own conscientious response, this threatens our sense of the true meaning of Church.

Law, bureaucracy, and tradition become humanized when used in the service of charity, in the building up of the Kingdom in our midst. Otherwise, they become dehumanized and dehumanizing by being co-opted into the service of fear and the compulsive need for tidiness and order, for the good of the corporate image at the expense of human dignity and freedom. Thus we need to keep constantly in mind the necessity of ongoing discernment as to how effectively celibacy is serving its designated purpose, the service of the virtue of religion.

The process of discernment takes place on an individual as well as a communal level. As one grows and develops through meeting and responding to various circumstances and experiences, new discoveries are made about oneself; there is growth in self-awareness. Not surprisingly, some of those discoveries will call into question previous assumptions and the decisions—however honest they might have been—based on those assumptions.

I do not advocate a casual attitude towards a stated public commitment to perpetual celibacy. Entering into any career requiring such a commitment is a serious matter, not one to be taken lightly. On the other hand, it is simplistic and unenlightened to continue believing that there are not going to be reasons and circumstances—not the least of which might be inadequate, careless or insensitive spiritual guidance during seminary years—in which some individuals will find perpetual celibacy impossible or undesireable.

If marriage is the desirable option for those people it should mean neither a diminishment in personal dignity nor a loss of the valuable resources they represent. Marriage is the sacrament wherein God continues his self-revelation through human cooperation; it should be the focal point wherein Eucharistic celebration finds its ultimate expression in human relationships, established and bonded together in the Eucharistic love of Christ. Eucharistic celebrations in the larger community might achieve a whole new dimension of meaning if married as well as celibate ministers were the presiders of the Eucharistic Liturgy. The supreme value proclaimed throughout our Sacred Scriptures is the value and sacredness of the intimate relationship that exists between God and the individual soul. The most reprehensible wrong that can happen in a community is in law, human traditions, and institutional bureaucracy becoming insensitive to that primary value, setting other interests and concerns above those of the person and his or her personal response to God. In this connection, we should consider the harsh words Christ had for those who laid heavy burdens on the shoulders of others without lifting a finger to help carry the load (Mt. 23.4). The strength and life of a community emerge from reverence for the individual and for the particular gifts that he or she has to give. Therefore, laws and customs must always serve the process that brings to birth and fruition the life of God in each person. Only then can a person truly give himself or herself as gift to the community.

We must recognize the enormity of the scandal of our individual and corporate attitudes that accept the status quo in which former priests are relegated to the margins of our Church community or even are positively excluded because of the unreasonable burdens that we, as a church, have laid on them. Under the present system, ordinaries and religious superiors find themselves in the contradictory position of having their judgments usually based on firsthand information, second-guessed by indifferent bureaucrats in Rome. The ones deemed competent to call men to priesthood, to oversee their training, to evaluate their readiness and fitness for the office, and, finally to ordain them are required to surrender their personal judgment and opinions to others in distant places, who know little of the individual circumstances. If we are to be worthy of the mission of the Church to the world, we must examine our attitudes to see how we can offer compassion to our brothers who wait to be called back into the mainstream of Catholic life and worship. This is a responsibility of both the laity and bishops, pastors and religious superiors.

The scandal is compounded most ironically when men who have been called and anointed by the Church to be witnesses of the sacrament of matrimony and to uphold the sacredness of its sacramental character are themselves, because of church policy, placed in the predicament of having no choice but to enter into a marriage contract that the Church considers illicit and invalid. At the same time, bishops and religious superiors of clerical men are drawn into a totally intolerable situation in which obedience to curial policy places them in direct opposition to obedience to the highest values of the church: charity and its first fruit, compassion. All of this is caused by an arbitrary choice to make human law and tradition the supreme value of a Church founded on the One who came to heal and to reconcile.

Compassion and charity, to say nothing of justice, require that Church leadership provide affirmation and support in a way of life that offers new promise for their brothers, as well as for the Church community. Otherwise, the Shepherds bear reponsibility for having abdicated their role over those whom they have called to assist them in their ministry. That is to say nothing of the scandal given to many who measure the credibility and moral authority of the Church not by sophisticated legal, logical or theological reasonings, but by an intuitive knowledge of right and wrong, of justice and charity.

There is little doubt that we are privileged to be living in a time of speedy and dramatic transition, not only in the church but in all aspects of society. The changes we see taking place around us today are undoubtedly going to have a dramatic impact on our sense of what it means to be church with a message of promise to our time. Even as we experience some anxiety over the apparent inadequacy of many of our accustomed methods of penetrating and bringing light and direction to the confusion of our society, the discerning person will be able to perceive new, if quiet and subtle, signs of new life.

From many quarters we hear prophecies of gloom about the future of religious life and the celibate priesthood. As is often the case however, even while some are convinced we are seeing the end of religious life and a celibate priesthood as we have known them, there are signs that increasing numbers of the faithful are beginning to realize and appreciate the inherent value contained within these traditions. We are learning a lesson that we are too prone to forget. Namely, that throughout the ages the Spirit of God confounds human wisdom by breathing life where, for all intents and purposes, there appears to be only death. The Spirit breathes life where others see only dry bones. As religious communities struggle with decreasing numbers, new forms of community living begin to take shape. Characteristically these communities share a common dedication to living a life of Evangelical simplicity, commitment to prayer and the study and implementation of the values of Sacred Scripture in their work place. These new forms, while still small in number and relatively insignificant in influence, show every sign of meeting the needs of a growing number of the Catholic Faithful, as well as a society sorely in need of a prophetic witness to alternatives and solutions to the confusion and darkness evident around us.

It is not uncommon today to encounter young men or women who have spent time in monastic communities following the regular routine of prayer and work without ever intending to remain as permanent members. With the consent of the host community, they availed themselves of the opportunity to learn about prayer, silence, and traditional ascetical practices in order to return to the world strengthened in their spiritual life and fortified with a resolve to live the Gospel in simplicity and obscurity in the midst of the secular society. In some instances these people attempt to enter support groups to take the place of the monastic community, but many remain alone, attached to a spiritual director or one or two companions with whom they pray and study scripture even as they continue their trades or professions. In some instances these people maintain a loose connection with their host monastic community by returning from time to time for periods of prayer and community support.

As I have travelled around the United States and Canada, I have encountered married couples of all ages who show an uncommon interest in deepening their prayer and knowledge of Sacred Scripture as a way of adding depth and meaning to their lives as parents or professionals in the work place. Throughout the Church in North America there is a growing desire to get beneath the surface of religious practice to the life-giving waters of Sacred Scripture and a personal relationship with the Creator.

In these unofficial and relatively unnoticed little groupings grounded in deep prayer and commitment to living radically the Evangelical Counsels, I believe God's Spirit is breathing new life into the Church and the world. For many of these people celibacy is a very real option. Some young persons seriously consider celibacy as a viable option while not necessarily seeing this as a decision to enter seminary or relgous life. Others who have experienced divorce or separation see a commitment to celibacy as a viable option to remarriage. In almost all cases I have seen, this decision is made in connection with a perceived call to live a more radical life of prayer and simplicity of life style connected with service in the world. A common thread running throughout is that, whether celibate or married, there appears to have been a conversion experience enabling them to see the futility of so many of their pursuits. They have tasted of the pleasures—and stresses—of the world, and found them wanting. Thus, these persons are marked by a maturity and self-possession born of of experience. They are marked by a sense of responsibility that prompts them to pursue the Wisdom of the Gospel—the Wisdom that appears as folly to those whose eyes remain closed.

The heartening message here is that while on one level we see our society entangled in a disheartening and sickening fascination with self-aggrandizement, hedonistic pursuits and the acquisition of manipulative power, there is a very quiet and unheralded revolution moving many toward a re-examination of Gospel values and traditional ascetical principles that have time and again drawn us away from the abyss of self destruction.

Perhaps once again we are about to witness the power of God's Spirit working in harmony with human spirits open and docile to a higher wisdom than this world has to offer. Again we would witness the silent mystery of God's Holy Spirit wending its way between the pillars of human wisdom and power ensconced in Church and State, quietly and gently probing and searching out the obscure and humble hearts of this world.

Perhaps in this subtle and silent movement of God's Spirit operating in synergy with the human spirit, we will see the re-emergence of Christian community comprised of married couples living in supportive relationships with celibate men and women. There is no reason to assume that those who are celibate will see this as a permanent state of life. Some might find a temporary commitment to celibacy within a community setting a stabalizing influence during a part of their spiritual development. Some, on the other hand, might come to realize that they are called to make a lifetime commitment to celibacy. At any rate, these communities will provide a healthy setting in which men and women will find support in prayer and friendship to make life's choices that will benefit them as well as the larger Church community. In this way we can hope to see the re-emergence of celibacy as a powerful and bold statement to the world from within the heart of the Church.